Amazing Tales

of St. Lawrence Neighbourhood

BRUCE BELL

Bruce Bell

Chapter Index

Bruce Bell

Photo and Illustration Index

Bruce Bell

PARADISE SOUGHT

Starving 10-year-old boys were hanged for stealing cookies. It was what seemed like justice to early residents of what is now Toronto. It was, in those days, a stinking muddy hell of flies and pestilence in the summer and of frozen want in winter. It was ruled over by haughty aristocrats who believed they were ordained by Heaven to impose their boots on the people.

Most of our pioneers suffered privation to bring us what we now cherish and strive to improve. That is still the story of Toronto as immigrants from around the world constantly renew us.

Where we live makes an impression on us. Perhaps psychically it also influences us. So there is a natural desire to learn the history of one's home.

Ours in St. Lawrence Neighbourhood is both ancient and modern.

In 1979 a large part of this historic area that was by then industrial wasteland was—by the will of the city—transmogrified into a neighbourhood. The concept was to create an urban residential scheme largely on the order of what urban philosopher Jane Jacobs promoted.

The residences were to be largely mixed with all the urban types living harmoniously together. In co-operatives, city-owned rentals, condominiums and freehold townhouses, the new St. Lawrence Neighbourhood housed the rich, the poor and the middle class of all colours, stripes and creeds.

It worked almost better than hoped. St. Lawrence Neighbourhood quickly became an example shown to the world by urban planners of nearly ideal urban residential planning.

There is no more passionate a pursuer of our history than Bruce Bell. A professional showman, he has inserted his flair for the dramatic into a love of our history that has regaled readers of his regular monthly history columns in the St. Lawrence Neighbourhood *Community Bulletin*, which I edit.

It has not been an unrequited love. Bruce has been loved back by Toronto and especially by this Neighbourhood. This book contains a collection of his columns, some reworked to reflect changes since they were written, and old photos from the City of Toronto Archives, some of which are published for the first time.

The faces of our Neighbourhood have changed dramatically since it was hacked out of the forest. Waves of immigrants have made it so.

From their endurance no doubt springs Toronto's sense of destiny delayed; of a blooming glory not fully recognized beyond our borders and just about to be fulfilled in a few finishing strokes next year. Or next.

Frank Touby
40 Henry Lane Terrace
Toronto
November 24, 2001

Special thanks go to neighbour Elisabeth Horley-McLeod, a teacher, who rushed through with copyediting and proof reading in time to hold to a minimum any errors in this book.

Published by
Community Bulletin Newspaper Group, Inc.
121-260 Adelaide Street East
Toronto, Ontario M5A 1N1
(416) 368-3071 cbnews@canada.com

PRINTED IN CANADA

TORONTO STARTED HERE

The history of the St. Lawrence Neighbourhood is the history of Toronto. Not only are its boundaries home to the original eighteenth-century colonial settlement of the Town of York. But those same streets would later become the centre of Victorian life in nineteenth-century Toronto. Two hundred years ago we saw the first commercial wharves built at the foot of Church Street and at the same time just up the street witnessed the first church being erected.

We were home to York's first markets and town hall that later would serve as Toronto's first city hall.

We were invaded by the Americans during the War of 1812 (which Canada won) and shook our fists as the "Yanks" set fire to our parliament buildings at Parliament and King, where recent archeological digs show there is much worth preserving on the site.

We were there when the railroad came through in the 1850s and saw the building of the great warehouses that were to be filled with all the goods a vibrant city would need. We became home to thousands of Irish immigrants fleeing the Great Potato famine and all of us stood in terror when the old town of York went up in flames in 1849. A new city would be built from those ashes, a city that would rise in imperial dignity to be the envy of the world.

That city—the very model for the rest of the British Empire—after sinking into a twentieth-century industrialized wasteland would once again rise from the ashes to become the St. Lawrence Neighbourhood, our home.

These stories are about the buildings, businesses, hotels, banks and theatres, and most importantly the people who at one time occupied the streets we now call home. Ironically many of the twentieth-century businesses I write about are now history themselves like the demise of the Cineplex movie theatre or the fact that the new A&P Front Street Market already has an even newer first name: Dominion. So fast is progress.

To those who come to live here after we have departed: May you learn not only of our things but also of us.

Bruce Bell
Performing Arts Lodge
St. Lawrence Neighbourhood
Toronto
November 17, 2001

Dedication

To my brother Mark who never stopped believing in me.

Bruce Bell

MARKET ALWAYS A FOCUS FOR PASSIONS

A crowd of angry citizens who wanted to keep the landmark Market shouted down the city planners.

FRONT STREET EAST 1953— north side, east of Jarvis. Notice the great shed (far left) that at one time connected the north and south markets.

St. Lawrence Market is without a doubt the cornerstone and historic heart of our Neighbourhood. It defines who we are, at least territorially. The massive building that stands on the corner of Jarvis and Front has been through it all.

The Market didn't always look like it does today, it's been re-built, re-modeled, rejuvenated and re-vamped more times than Cher's career. In its 156-year history it's been home to a city hall, a fisherman's wharf, a police station and a jailhouse. It survived the Great Fire of 1849 and has almost been demolished twice.

The story of the Market is the story of Toronto.

In 1834, the year we went from being the Town of York to the City of Toronto, we had a population of 9,000. By 1844 it grew to over 24,000 and with this new expansion came fresh cash and a decision to construct a new city hall.

A competition was held, as was the custom when public buildings were constructed, and the winner was Henry Bowyer Joseph Lane. He was a member of the infamous ruling elite called the Family Compact (his aunt had married one of the Boulton family, builders of the Grange) which held power over practically everything and everybody that was in Toronto at the time. Lane was only in Toronto four years (1843-1847) but in that time managed to build Little Trinity Church on King, additions to Osgoode Hall and Holy Trinity Church behind the Eaton Centre.

What I find interesting in looking at the old photographs of Lane's design, is that his hall wasn't very bold or daring, considering we had just become a city. It has the look of an overly ambitious fire station. In 1852, W.H. Smith wrote in his book, *Canada: Past, Present and Future*, the following criticism: "A very strange-looking building and it was unfortunate for the reputation of the architect that he had not left the province before he completed the building instead of afterwards…"

11

Had one of the other proposals been chosen instead, we might have today a stunning miniature replica of Rome's Pantheon or Washington's Capitol Dome on the southwest corner of Jarvis and Front. Maybe it was his connections that got him the commission (it did cause an uproar from the other architects) but his was the less expensive design.

So in 1844, on land where the Home District Farmer's Storehouse once stood, work began on the new and desperately needed city hall. Up until then, the city council was crammed in above the old Market (on the site of the present day St. Lawrence Hall) in the former town chambers, which would serve as our first city hall after incorporation.

That old Market (1832-1849) was, like the chambers, becoming overcrowded and unsanitary what with all the pig slop and out-in-the-open butchering going on. (Before refrigeration, I definitely would have become a vegetarian).

Construction of the new city hall was spurred on by the building of Kingston's palatial city hall. Toronto, after losing its status as the capital city of the United Canada to Kingston in 1841, chose instead to be an economic powerhouse. A new city hall complete with a police station, a jail and newer market facilities for poultry and fish on the edge of the then harbour was just the thing.

Building it on the waterfront would give the new hall an impressive appearance as ships rounded the bay: "There, in all its splendour, the new City of Toronto and its centre, its grand city hall." The city hall did look better from the lake, it stood out amongst the wharves and piers that lined what would become The Esplanade and rising from its roof was a clock tower. Being situated so close to the waterfront would also produce one of our Neighbourhood's greatest urban legends: the horrors of the dungeon.

Where the main entrance to the Market is today, there was a foyer, a spiral staircase and a police office. The staircase led up to the second floor where, facing Front, the mayor had his office.

At the rear, overlooking the harbour on the second floor, was the council chamber. A third floor held the public gallery that looked down over the chambers. The two arches (the red doors were added in 1876) that flank the main entrance led to the Market stalls.

The basement was the domain of Police Station No. 1 and its infamous dungeon-like jails.

Before the days of prison reform and common-sense justice, people were thrown into that jail, chained to the wall (where Domino's coffee grinder is) and later executed, if so deemed, for as little as stealing a piece of candy. (It's ironic that today, many people sneak a nut or a piece of candy from the tempting open bins at Domino, not realizing how dangerous that would have been in earlier times.)

During a storm the waters of Lake Ontario would rise, flood the jail, and the helpless people shackled to the wall would drown or, at the very least, hang knee deep in all the contaminated debris washing up from the open sewer that was Lake Ontario. If those walls could talk, they'd scream.

Someone back then thinking this was barbaric or feeling sorry for the jail guards who had to mop up the gunk, decided to move the jail cells to the newly opened court house (1851) on Adelaide St. where today, in the basement of the brilliantly renovated Court House Restaurant, they can be seen.

When the Great Fire ripped through the downtown core in 1849, the new city hall was spared but the old Market across the street went up in flames. Like Atlanta after Sherman's March, we too rebuilt. A new Market was built and behind it, the St. Lawrence Town Hall, which still stands today.

In 1850, it was noticed that the city hall was sinking into the clay beneath its foundations.

The city hired architects William Thomas (St. Lawrence Town Hall) and John Howard (practically everything else) to re-configure the plan and stabilize it. They also added some ornamentation to the façade, giving Lane's original ho-hum building a splash of décor.

So for the next 50 years you could walk through the town hall on King; enter the new Market, come out onto Front, cross the street, set foot in city hall, descend to the lower level, pick out some fruits and vegetables from the shops that lined the open courtyard, continue to the back where the Market wharf once stood (today the site of Pontieri's Auto Centre) and buy your freshly caught fish.

In 1860 the hall was vividly decorated for a royal visit when Edward, Prince of Wales, later Edward VII, dropped by for a reception.

By the late 1890s, Toronto was booming, its population was almost 200,000, and it was time to build yet another city hall. The question was, what to do with the old one?

A Market commission was formed and they recommended to the city that the hall undergo a major renovation, which would last from 1899 to 1901. The architect chosen, John Siddall, decided to do away with the east and west wings and remove the clock tower but rather than tearing down the entire city hall he instead created a treasure enclosed within a legend.

Amazing Tales of St. Lawrence Neighbourhood

If you stand facing St. Lawrence Market from across the street you can still see the yellow brick outline that was the centre block of our second city hall.

Of course, you can get a better view from inside the Market. That centre block, once the home to the council chambers and now the Toronto Archive Art Gallery is a wonderment of reclamation. If only more of this type of restoration was done instead of absolute annihilation, our Neighbourhood would have become a world-renowned architectural treasure on the same rank of Quebec City or Prague.

With its graceful arches, hidden alcoves and the great fan window that looms over the inside of the Market, the former council chamber is a reminder that unfashionable and dated structures need not be discarded so hastily.

Siddall placed an enormous roof (known as Siddall Shed) over the new building, built supporting trusses to hold it and raised the council chamber floor to allow more height over the main entrance.

Unfortunately he and city planners also decided to tear down the masterpiece of Victorian splendour that was the market across the street and built the forerunner to the present day North or Farmers Market.

So the Neighbourhood was to get two markets, north and south, with an enormous canopy spanning Front Street connecting the pair. The two markets were built to complement each other but the North Market (1904-68) failed to have any of the architectural histrionics the South Market had going for it. It was a colossal barn that butted up against St. Lawrence Town Hall destroying the hall's elegant outline.

I'm only going by old photographs and probably when built the old North Market looked quite agreeable, having the same intricate brick buttress-truss system holding up its roof. Unlike the South Market, it was allowed to deteriorate and was ultimately demolished in 1968.

In 1901 with the huge connecting canopy (which lasted until 1954) preventing any light from entering the street below together with the polluting gasoline engine making its appearance, the whole area now devoid of any picturesque vistas, the St. Lawrence Market opened for business. Our Neighbourhood, once quaintly known as Muddy York, began its descent into an urban rotting hell.

Recently I took a tour along the catwalk that hangs below the roof to get a closer look. As frightening as it was to be suspended so high up with only an open grid of steel between me and the Market floor four stories below, seeing the intricate iron workings of Siddall Shed was breathtaking. Here is Victorian Industrialism at its height. The rivets, pounded in by men long since departed together with arcs of steel symbolizing the Industrial Revolution itself crisscrossing the ceiling, have all the beauty and power of the Vatican's Sistine Chapel but instead of paint its medium is iron.

Seventy years later it was time to do another restoration job on the building I like to call my corner store.

In 1971, the city's planning board and a consultant's report had proposed that the South Market be demolished. The shocking claim here is, I can't believe what with Toronto's penchant for exterminating all things historic, that the Market managed to survive up to the 1970s!

At a public meeting held in the fall of 1971 something extraordinary happened, a crowd of angry citizens who wanted to keep the landmark Market shouted down the city planners. The long-suppressed voice of a citizens-led movement that was years in the making was finally being heard.

In the 1890s, the preservation movement got started when anger arose over the fact that graves of the War of 1812 soldiers were being dug up and used as landfill during the building of the railroad lands on the site of the most historic spot in Toronto, Fort York.

In 1905 a teacher, Jean Geeson, continued the fight to save, after years of being slowly whittled away, what was left of the fort. In the late 1950s, during the building of the oppressive Gardiner Expressway, some mindless bureaucrat wanted to tear down Fort York so the expressway could flow in a straight line rather than curve to avoid the fort. He lost and the movement started up again, then evolved into The Toronto Historical Board.

In 1969, John Sewell, running for city council, used as a political poster a picture of himself standing amongst the rumble of a demolished building with a caption reading, "When will this stop?"

The group who wanted to save St. Lawrence Market called themselves "Time and Place" and they recommended that it be renovated and the council chamber, which sat unused for 70 years, turned into a public gallery.

So with money from all three forms of government in place, the outside was cleaned, a new floor was poured, the brick piers supporting the roof trusses were re-enforced, and one half of the roof was replaced.

Downstairs, which once housed the former jails and later was used for wholesale storage and the unloading of trucks, was gutted and refurbished. After years of being covered up and forgotten, the original foundation bricks and graceful vaulted arches were exposed that today skip above our heads as we shop at Phil's or buy rice at Rube's or grind our coffee at Everyday Gourmet on the lower level.

Never meant as ornamentation, they have managed to survive and are one of the many riches the Market has to offer. Without the St. Lawrence Market, our Neighbourhood and Toronto itself would be humbled. There was talk, after the opening of the huge Loblaws supermarket, of the Market going under. What with losing its parking spaces to new condo sites, competition from the food giant and the more recent 24-hour Dominion Front Street Market, rumours abound. They always do.

Still, the Market thrives and heartens all who visit whether they're once-a-week Friday or Saturday shoppers, monthly visitors, or those most fortunate of us who can drop in several times a week. I'm sure it will never be threatened with closure. But if it should be, in memory of those before me, I will chain myself to the front door—along with nearly everyone else in the Neighbourhood…and most of Toronto!

SOUTH SIDE OF FRONT STREET EAST 1952—The warehouses and Market are still standing (minus the Great Shed). The picture is taken in front of what is now the liquor store.

OUR SOBRIETY WAS MYTHICALLY EPIC

Sometimes selling her body was the only way
a woman left on her own could make any money

ONTARIO CHAMBERS BUILDING 1873—northeast corner of Front and Church. Now the site of the famous Hot House Café in Market Square.

The land that Market Square now occupies (north side of Front between Church Street and Market Lane Park), was at one time the home of bohemian life in old York. It's also been the site of Toronto's first live theatre, numerous taverns, inns, hotels, a murder involving an associate of William Lyon Mackenzie and a brothel or two. And that was only by 1830.

Market Square, and its newest tenant The Front Street Market, sits on land that was originally part of the first plan of York, laid out by Simcoe and his men in 1793 and like so much of our Neighbourhood, its history goes back even farther. For thousands of years previous, during the fishing season, the Huron first nation would make camp by a small creek that wound its way down to the Lake. For centuries the land now dominated by the Market Square Condos, Cineplex, Harvey's, A&P and the St. Lawrence Markets (North and South) was at one time the summer home to generations of Canada's First People. That now-buried creek and its subsequent fishing is the reason the St. Lawrence Market, let alone Toronto, was built where it is.

Front Street in the late 1700s was a wide dirt road and the area in front of the present day A&P was an open field edging on the lake. One of the first structures the Europeans built on that site upon arriving here was a hotel and it quickly became the focal point of the city. The Steamboat Hotel, so named because its façade was shaped like a steamboat, was located approximately where the main doors to the A&P now stand. (From the 1860s to the 1960s the north side of Front Street between Church and West Market Street was a series of nondescript but highly useful buildings designed to be part of the St. Lawrence Market complex, with the exception of course of the former Ontario Chambers Building.)

Ulick Howard built his hotel in 1827 after selling his Farmers Arms Hotel, which was connected to the Market next door. The Steamboat Hotel had an unobstructed view of the lake and guests would gather along its second floor balcony and watch what must have been magnificent sunsets. It would be another 25 years before the warehouses that today stand across the street would be built. On June 19, 1828 a circus came to town called the "Grand Caravan of Living Animals" and it was held in the ballroom of the hotel. The poster of the day announced "... the great African lion, the lioness, South American tiger and jaguar, the camel, the leopard, the young llama, baboons, monkeys, a variety in all consisting of about thirty curiosities in natural history will be exhibited at Mr. Howard's Steamboat Hotel..." The following week a group of traveling musicians from Germany with a 21 century-sounding name—"The Androides: A Grand Musical Machine"—arrived and they in turn were followed by "The Extra Ordinary Exhibition of the Industrial Fleas of England." The Steamboat, or Howard's Hotel (and later, after incorporation, the City Hotel as it was commonly known), was also the place where powerful government gentlemen of the day would converged after elections to kick up their heels. On July 12, 1828 after the victorious return to power a party was given to honour John Robinson as attorney general. He was paraded through the streets of York, held high on a chair amidst music and cheering. The men wound up at the hotel where Mr. Howard put on a show of music and entertainment and they drank themselves silly.

How Toronto got a reputation for being boring is a mystery if all this was going on during a few weeks in the summer of 1828. It could be that the social, religious and bureaucratic leaders of the day went out of their way to make the world think we were a sober lot. It made them, look better. Toronto was anything but boring; we were as wild as San Francisco. We were bound to be, with no decent roads leading in or out of town (most travel came by water) and being stuck in the middle of nowhere the more daring town's folk had to do something to off-set boredom. They started to congregate around the Market and subsequently the centre of all things hip, 1800s style, became the area bounded by Front, Jarvis, King and Church Streets named then, as is it is now, Market Square. The rich and titled townsfolk had their own amusements, usually discussing the goings on of those they felt they were superior to and generally hung out at Jordan's Hotel near the Parliament Buildings at Berkeley and Front Streets. One thing is known, both groups drank heavily and liked to party, wink-wink. With a population of about 6,000 in 1830 there were 60 taverns and as many brothels. A brothel could be a few rooms above an Inn or the back room of someone's house. It was commonly known that if an establishment had a sign above its door that read, "Oysters and hot coffee always ready," it meant that an available prostitute was on call. The red-light district in the early days of York centred around Church and Front, and the most infamous house of prostitution stood where Pizza Pizza now stands. Sometimes selling one's body was the only way a woman, left on her own, could make any money. Though she could never enter high social circles (or probably ever wanted to) she was, if discreet, left alone. It was the men of the day who visited her who were publicly shamed. In an editorial in a local newspaper. *The Canadian Freeman*, dated May 26, 1831,

FRONT AND CHURCH 1955—site of Market Square.

Francis Collins (there is a plaque dedicated to him in St. James Park) writes the following:

"Houses of infamy are scattered thro' every corner of the town and one of them had the hardihood to commence operations next door to our office. Young lawyers and others of respectable standing, crowd to it at noonday and some of them visited it in open day and on the Sabbath! We had no idea that such depravity existed in our infant community. Such men should be viewed as a walking pestilence and scouted out of all decent society. Some of our authorities and heads of families too visit debauchery of this kind which if not checked will suffer the wrath of God..." That is how York wanted to be perceived, terrible things written about in an unhanded manner. But at the same time in a rival newspaper, *The Colonial Advocate* (William Lyon Mackenzie's paper), a letter signed Glendocharty states the following:

"In a town with an assortment of stores, auction rooms, hotels, taverns, inns, oyster shops (establishments consecrated to sex for hire), the midnight customer walks into artificial darkness and doze away their time in the arms of intoxication or pay their adoration to the enchanting goddess of licentiousness and debauchery." That surprises me because as great a man and as left wing as William was, one thing he wasn't was a bohemian; he probably let that ditty be printed because he hated the status quo regardless of his own views on the matter. On the other side of Market Square where the entrance to Cineplex now stands, facing that poor excuse for a park, there was an establishment called Frank's Tavern. In that tavern in 1820 Toronto's theatrical debut took place. That was the place to go if you wanted to be part of the in crowd. Men and women dressed in the latest French fashions together with off-duty soldiers from Fort York looking for a little bit of off-hours action all gathered to be entertained by local actors.

As the beer-drenched evening progressed the actors, now standing on tabletops, began to recite Shakespeare for all to hear, on the site where today we line up to buy our movie tickets. A night at Frank's was the topic you'd talk about the next day to your neighbour as you went about slaughtering your pig.

There is a story of a titled lady, Mary Willis, who lived at Frank's hotel while waiting for her house to built and she wouldn't leave her room because she wasn't properly introduced to the other titled ladies of the town. They wouldn't visit her because they felt she should make the first move. And so she sat. It took an act of outrageous decorum by the titled gentlemen of the town and research from the book, Established Etiquette in the Colony, to bring these ladies together. Protocol was everything to aristocracy of early York. Give me the actor's life any day. Next door to Frank's stood another, more infamous nightspot, The Colborne Theatre,

CITY ARMS HOTEL 1952— West side of Market Street between Front and King; now the site of Market Square and the former lobby to the Cineplex.

where A&P's frozen food section now resides. In 1829 a murder took place outside the theatre involving one of Mackenzie apprentices, Charles French. After a performance, French, in a drunken state, confronted and stabbed a man named Nolan who was well known as the town's bully. The feeling at the time was, "good for French," but the law of the time deemed that "French be hanged for his crime," which he was. All theatrical performances in York were banned until further notice. A few years later, in 1833, a group of actors descended upon our town and preceded to put on a performance that evolved into a wild party and lasted well into the wee hours of the morning in a tavern near the Market and caused our hero William Lyon Mackenzie to write the following in his newspaper:

"Our town has been infested several weeks past with a company of strolling players issuing their handbills of monkey-shines purporting to be theatrical performances.

"We were particularly disgusted with a playbill for last Saturday night. Only think of allowing such a party of strolling vagrants to keep a giddy party of foolish people up on Saturday night perhaps two or three o'clock upon Sabbath morning. We wonder they have not been arrested under the vagrant act and banished out of the town long ago. Clear the vagabonds out at once and free the town from a nuisance!" Maybe because an associate of his, who was involved with actors, was hanged, Mackenzie had it in for actors and theatre in general. In 1837 Mackenzie led his ill-fated rebellion against the ruling elite and was himself banished to the 'States before returning to a hero's welcome 10 years later.

The area that now houses Market Square flourished with exotic delights during the first half of the nineteenth century. In the early morning of April 7, 1849 a fire ripped through the area destroying not only the buildings but also a way of life. All was lost. The Market, that brought people to the area to begin with, the hotels where people stayed, the theatre where players performed and patrons came to be entertained and the taverns where the unrelenting boredom of a winter's night could be broken, all gone in a night of unimaginable horror. It's ironic that the Great Fire should have happened during Queen Victoria's reign, when all things—on the outside at least—suddenly and forcibly became respectable. Toronto would become the ideal of British respectability. The spires on its cathedrals would become the highest points in the city, the facades of buildings would become the ideal of Victorian architecture and the manner of its people, at any cost, would become the envy of the Empire.

Whatever promise Toronto was beginning to show as an individualist city with its own unique identity—in spite of the ruling classes' desperate need to create a miniature London, England—was lost in the Great Fire.

We had to belong, we were not under any circumstances going to be anything but a model of Victorian idealism and especially we were not going to be Americanized. Besides, a clean living Methodist city was good for business. For the next hundred years those who were deemed "different" suffered at the hands of those who tried to live up to an impossible-to-maintain illusion. So with Victoria cemented on her throne and Toronto's elite still in power despite Mackenzie's war, a new block of buildings went up on the site of the Steamboat Hotel, Frank's Tavern and the Colborne Theatre.

Tremendous growth from the 1850s onward resulted in a huge building boom. From the 1860s to the 1960s the north side of Front Street between Church and West Market Street was a series of nondescript but highly useful buildings designed to be part of the St. Lawrence Market complex. Mostly used for warehousing and poultry manufacturing, the area that at one time was the centre of all things cool in the early 1800s had gone the way of progress. In the late 1960s that site too came crashing down and the area became a parking lot before the building of Market Square in 1982. In 1967 the city during the madness of urban renewal decided to do away with West Market Street. They replaced it with Market Lane Park (named for a laneway that once ran through the area) and in doing so they destroyed a very valuable piece of our history. It wouldn't be so bad if they had indeed built a park with grass but instead chose lay concrete and plant what is arguably the most hideous garden, we have in the city. All throughout the nineteenth and twentieth centuries West Market Street was a hub of activity. Horse drawn wagons and later trucks filled with produce lined the street and outdoor vendors hocked their wares. Up until the 1830s it's where the town crier would dispense royal proclamations or shout-out the latest news and where helpless people, their heads locked in stocks for crimes ranging from stealing bread to 'wanton acts of impurity' would be on view. Every block, every street, every piece of land we have in our Neighbourhood has some historical significance and Market Square is brimming.

The next time you're strolling through the Front Street Market, picking out fruit and vegetables, take time to listen to the ghosts. Hear our political past toasting and cheering, the roar of the lion, the ever-popular European music sensations The Androids, the actor's romantic soliloquy and the silent cry of prostitutes and titled ladies. We are walking on the shoulders of the dead. More than ever it proves that we aren't just any Neighbourhood in Toronto, we are The Neighbourhood.

OUR HAUNTED HOUSE

The city's first taxi service was started by a former American slave.

Was it just luck, or something else that has kept the building on the southeast corner of Sherbourne and Adelaide still in existence? At present its totally unrecognizable but underneath all that red paint and patchy brickwork sits a fine Georgian house first built in 1842 by blacksmith extraordinaire, Paul Bishop. He built his house upon the foundations of one of the most famous manor homes of old York and consequently it now occupies some of the most historic land in the city.

Paul Bishop's house went on to miraculously survive the Great Fire of 1849, the onslaught of the Industrial Revolution and the horrors of the 1960's Urban Renewal. Thanks to a city agreement with developers, this historic house will be restored back to its early nineteenth century splendour as part of the deal for a new condo on the northeast corner of King and Sherbourne to be known as Kings Court. In 1793, the year of our European founding, what was to become the southeast corner of Sherbourne and Adelaide was still part of a great forest. There was a small stream running into Lake Ontario, which then came up as far as Front Street, and the only buildings in the area were a few canvas and wooden huts hastily set up by the Queens Rangers in preparation of Gov. Simcoe's arrival. In 1798 one of those Queens Rangers, William Jarvis, having liked this corner of the new capital of Upper Canada (now called York) so much that he built a small villa on what would become the four corners of Sherbourne and Adelaide and named it Jarvis House—after himself, naturally. The house built of squared logs was 30 by 41 feet, had two floors and was covered with clapboarding. The only major exterior detail was a fanlight over the front door. William, the provincial secretary and registrar from before Simcoe's arrival in 1793 until his death in 1818, decided not to spend too much money on the outside in case he was forced to sell if the capital was to move to London. The house sat on two acres spread over the entire Sherbourne and Adelaide area. The estate held two barns, a root house, a stable, a chicken coup and (like homes of the rest of our well-to-do founding fathers) had slave quarters built to house the six people he owned.

PAUL BISHOP'S HOUSE 1885—southeast corner of Sherbourne and Adelaide streets first built in 1848.

After William Jarvis died in 1817 his son cut the house and grounds into smaller sections. The house itself was taken over by a man named Lee who turned it into a restaurant and billiard room and added a small addition. In 1821 James Padfield rented a portion of the building and started a school. When the school was disbanded in 1824 Isaac Columbus took possession of the property and converted one part into workshops and the rest into his home. During the War of 1812 Isaac, a native of France, made swords and guns for our side at his forge near Fort York. Described as a "real character" by nineteenth-century historian Henry Scadding, he remembers telling Columbus that a specific item "must" be ready by a particular hour. Columbus staring him down with a terrifying glare reminded Scadding that only the king of France can use the term "must." Isaac hated the liberals of early Toronto because he believed that modern ideas "hindered the king from acting as a good father to his people." In 1832 Isaac moves out and James Kidd moves in.

It was during this time that the Jarvis House, as it was still known, became famous for unearthly reasons. During the cholera epidemics of the 1830s several people died in the house, including a few by suicide. Room after room was then being sealed shut to prevent cholera's spread. Townsfolk began to talk: "There's something not right at the old Jarvis House." One dark and stormy night James Kidd hears unnatural noises coming from Secretary Jarvis' office, boarded up ever since it was believed to be haunted. So with a pistol in one hand, a crow bar in the other and lightning striking a ghostly silhouette upon the wall, Kidd begins to pry open the door but as he does the noises stop.

In an age when Frankenstein the novel was a huge hit, stories like this had a life all their own. A few days later a man by the name of Baxter arrives to spend the night at Jarvis House. Kidd, hoping to solve the mystery, assigned Baxter the haunted room. During the night, it is recorded that "sounds of fury and noises never heard on this earth" emanated from the haunted room. The next morning a haggard Mr. Baxter appears at breakfast with suitcase in hand telling all present, "I will never pass another night in that room let alone this house, Good day." Some believed the apparition might have been that of John Ridout who was shot and killed in a duel by Samuel Jarvis, son of William, in 1817. To this day many believe his spirit, whose family had an estate next door, still floats about the Sherbourne and Adelaide area in search of his grave. (Oh yeah: I forgot to tell you, both families had private burial grounds in their back yards.) In 1842 James Kidd sells the house to Paul Bishop on the condition that he be allowed to live there until he dies. He dies a year later and in 1848 Paul Bishop tears down the old Jarvis House and builds upon the foundations the structure that still stands, in part, today. Bishop (a French Canadian whose real name L'Eveque meaning "the Bishop") was anglicized upon his arrival in Upper Canada. He established himself as a first-class blacksmith, locksmith and wheel maker. He was also the son in law of previous owner Isaac Columbus. Before taking ownership Bishop had his workshop across the street on the northeast corner (today the site of the jazz giant Montreal Bistro).

A few years before, in 1834, the year of incorporation, Thornton Blackburn came from the United States and worked as a waiter in Osgoode Hall. Then, in 1837, the always-inventive Blackburn made history by taking a pattern of a horse-drawn taxicab known then only to Montreal and London (UK) to Paul Bishop's workshop. It was there in his shed that Bishop built for Blackburn the first horse-drawn taxicab in Upper Canada. At a time when the United States was still torturing and enslaving a tenth of their population we here in Toronto had as our first taxicab owner a runaway American slave. The foundations of the house that Thornton and his wife Lucie lived in for over 50 years on Eastern Ave. near Cherry St. which served as a stop on the Underground Railroad have been recently been found and preserved. In 1860 Bishop, having built the house he lived in for almost 30 years, left town and disappeared from our history books. The house then came under the possession of Thomas Dennie Harris, one of leading merchants of the city, chief engineer of the fire brigade from 1838 to 1841 and harbour master from 1870 to 1872. Between 1841 and 1864 he was a warden of St. James' Church. Harris owned a hardware store since 1829 around the corner at 124 King East but it was destroyed during the Great Fire of 1849. Harris died in 1872 and with the encroachment of the Industrial Revolution upon this end of town the end was near for his home too. The small yard and fence that surrounded the house were torn up, as were the trees. Ironic because as warden of St. James one of Harris' duties was to protect the poplar trees that surrounded the church at the time. The great estates of the neighbourhood like the massive Moss Park (a story unto itself) up the street, the Ridout homestead next door and Russell Abbey down the street were being divided up and eventually demolished. The area once part of a great forest was to become for the next 100 years a polluted industrialized zone. The historic house at Sherbourne and Adelaide was stripped bare of its interior ornamentation, its windows bricked up, new doors were smashed through, its chimneys the very essence of its Georgian appeal though still standing were built upon and the grand memories of its former days just faded away. For the next 10 decades it became everything from a machine shop to a garage to a flophouse. It will return from the ashes to remind us all of our glorious past.

DUELS COULD BE DEADLY FOR WINNERS

'My dear, don't tell me your husband bought that gown for you.'

read a lot. Mostly it's about the history of the Neighbourhood we call home. But the more I read, the angrier I become. Why wasn't I, as a student attending a publicly funded school in Sudbury, taught any of what I'm now reading?

I want to go back to my hometown and sue the local school board for teaching me more about British monarchs and American presidents than, for example, the distinguished past of the area surrounding King and Parliament streets. How come I never knew that a sixteenth century revival of a French chateau that once stood on Power Street gave shelter and comfort to thousands of newly arrived immigrants for over 100 years?

How come I never knew about the eighteenth century explorer who, while canoeing his way on a now buried river trying to locate a way to the mythical Northwest Passage, found himself lost on what was to become the intersection of King and Parliament? He later told Simcoe that this would be the perfect place to build his new capital. Why was I never taught that? How come I know that 1600 Pennsylvania Avenue is the address to the American White House but never taught that 359 King East was once the centre of social and political life of Upper Canada? Furthermore, why are we allowing the very Swedish auto giant Volvo to build a dealership upon the site of our first Parliament buildings? Why is External Affairs, not to mention the Prime Minister's Office in Sweden, not answering any of my emails concerning this diplomatic oversight?

I ask myself: Why do I care? As beautifully produced and insightful as the CBC's Canada series was, it failed miserably when it came to telling Toronto's part in our country's history. Sure it gave us a few tidbits here and there but for the most part it chose instead to concentrate heavily on Quebec. Okay, I thought Quebec is older and maybe because of that it deserves more airtime. But the true insult to our history came when they substituted the ballroom of the St. Lawrence Hall for a ballroom in Quebec City during the Confederation episode. Doesn't that city have a ballroom grand enough to hold a dance in?

Why was there no mention or scenes of Sir John A. speaking in that very ballroom on the virtues of

HOUSE OF PROVIDENCE 1855—east side of Power St. between King and Queen East. Demolished in 1960 on/off Richmond Street ramp to the DVP and Gardiner.

Confederation? I could write another book just on how the CBC maligned us but I'll save that rant and concentrate on matters at hand. Why do I care? Because I live on land that has sown the seeds of a great nation and people who don't live here (and some who do) couldn't care less and that makes me mad. So toques off to the French Canadians! To them their history is worth fighting for and unlike ours comes to them through their mothers milk and the CBC. Back in 1793 or so, legend has it Lieutenant Givins (later colonel), out exploring what was to be the newly found town of York, took his canoe from the Bay of Toronto up what he thought was the mighty Don River. He, like many eighteenth-century explorers, was hoping to find a river that would lead to the Pacific and the fabled Northwest Passage. Instead he took a lesser stream, later named Goodwin's Creek which then came down from the north and crossed what are now King and Parliament streets. It was at that crossing where King Street has that dip'n turn that the flag was placed and the Town of York was born. Or so legend has it. But you'd never know it. There's nothing there to tell us.

Since the parliament buildings were built at the foot of present-day Berkeley Street, its name then was Parliament Street. (Yes, there is a plaque near the site but its wording is based on myth not fact. Very confusing when reading old maps.) Present day Parliament Street was a rough road leading up to Gov. Simcoe's country home, Castle Frank, overlooking the Don River at Bloor Street. Though he and his family lived at Fort York, occasionally they would venture up into the wilds of future Bloor Street to spend time in their canvas and wood cabin constructed to look like a Greek temple.

There was a small bridge crossing Goodwin's Creek which then ended King Street to become Kingston Road, or the road to Quebec, as it was then known. The first houses and businesses to spring up along that section were Mrs. Johnson's boarding house on the northwest corner of Ontario and King streets, Jordan's hotel on the south side opposite and behind that was a public oven operated by Paul Martin. This public bakery was in operation from at least 1804 until well after the Rebellion of 1837 for it is recorded that the bakery supplied bread to the militia forces of Toronto in 1839. Across from the hotel was the fabled Berkeley House on the southwest corner of King and Berkeley. The largest estate in the area was Maryville Lodge, home to D.W. Smith, the surveyor-general who came to Upper Canada with Simcoe. The estate took up the block bounded by King, Berkeley, Ontario and Adelaide streets and held up to 20 buildings including a stable with 13 stalls. Smith left York in 1804 and soon after Maryville lodge was demolished to make way for an expanding town.

Down the road on the present site of that slap-in-the-face-to-our-heritage former car wash where the parliament buildings first built in 1797. In 1794 John Small, the clerk of the executive council, constructed a modest home on the southwest corner of Berkeley and King. He built his house upon government-owned land,

BERKELEY HOUSE 1885—the home of John Small, southwest corner of Berkeley and King first built in 1794. Part of the estate is now the Toronto Sun parking lot.

which cause a minor scandal but nothing like the scandal that was to come.

Honour was everything back in the day and duels were often fought. At a government meeting the wife of the Attorney General John White said something to Mrs. Small that was taken as an insult. It could have been something as trivial as, "My dear don't tell me your husband bought that gown for you." It would be taken to mean some other man might have purchased it for her. Whatever was said, it forced the two husbands on Jan. 4, 1800 to defend the honour of their wives with a duel fought on what was then open ground fronting the lake just south of King on the west side of Parliament Street. Small won and White was dead. Small, having killed a member of the ruling class, was tried for murder but was later acquitted by the infamous Peter Russell who that same day had a Mr. Humphrey hung for stealing a forged note of one dollar. The Smalls were banned from society.

In a town that had a population of a present-day apartment building, banishment was seen as a worse punishment than hanging. In 1871 while workers were digging just north of the area they came across the bones of John White. Under the careful inspection and verification of a Clarke Gamble (White was buried in his backyard), the remains of poor White were removed to St. James' Cemetery. It makes me wonder who else is buried out there. The second generation of York's founders were not so heavily ruled by society niceties and would rather build industries and have fun than fight duels. Charles Small, son of John, inherited the modest home on the southwest corner of Berkeley and King, built an enormous addition (on what is now the Toronto Sun parking lot) and named the entire estate Berkeley House. The house, an Italian-styled villa, became the centre of social life in 1820s York. Carriages overflowing with young partygoers all dressed in the latest fashions would pull up nightly to the candle-lit house with what promised to be yet another evening of booze, laughter and political discussion. Their parents, whose own young lives were dictated to by a book known as Rules of Conduct in Upper Canada, could only just shake their heads.

In 1898 the original 1794 house was torn down and the present structure the Reid Brothers building (359 King E) was built. The Reid bros. also owned an enormous lumber factory complex at the bottom of Berkeley Street at the Esplanade.

The remaining addition to Berkeley House with its grand parlors, sweeping staircases and Italian Renaissance façade stood until 1926 when it too came crashing down after years of disuse. Across the street on the northeast corner of Berkeley and King and still standing was Garibaldi House (302 King E.) built as a hotel in 1859. Across from that on the northwest corner and also still standing is 300 King E. first built in 1845. Charles Small who lived across the street in Berkeley House once owned this and the still standing buildings attached. When this row was built it became the place for a gentleman to live while in town. The first tenants were Henry Sullivan a professor of anatomy at King's Collage, John Marling a local bon vivant and Charles' brother James who was the solicitor-general. In 1879 stores were added to the ground level and the addition—thrusting out onto the sidewalk still visible today at No. 300—was added.

It was then that one of Toronto's longest run family businesses, Greenshields Grocers, moved in and remained until 1956. The fourth corner, the one that now houses that white elephant known as the Business Depot was back when York was born an orchard next to an open field which doubled as the aforementioned dueling field. By at least 1878 the entire Staples (formerly Business Depot) block was taken over by the Hamilton Carriage Works makers of house drawn carriages. During the horses reign of power the entire area became a centre for horse and carriage makers. On the northwest corner of King and Parliament and still standing is the former home to Smith Bros. Carriage and Wagon Works first established in 1843. In need of a complete overhaul it is none the less a beautiful example of 19th century industrial workmanship plain and unadorned with just a hint of architectural detail. In its day the first floor was the blacksmith and iron working shop, the second was office space, the third was devoted to painting and trimming and the forth was their showroom. It was here that many of our first horse-drawn road washing wagons were built. I pray for the buildings continued survival.

Across the street on the northeast corner King and Parliament is the former home to the Aluminum and Crown Stopper Co. (334 King E.) built in 1912. This huge warehouse that at present time is having its back buildings knocked down is a community unto itself. I remember back in the 1990s having to walk up its eight flights of stairs to see a play at an experimental theatre, which during the day doubled as a friend's apartment. Across the street on land where the Derby apartment building now stands (393 King E.) was once the site of the Derby Tavern. Built in 1846 generations of Mill workers on their way home from a long day toiling at the various factories and mills in the area (like the still standing Gooderham and Worts) would stop off at the Derby. Once inside they would throw back tankards of ale and sing songs of the old country till they were blue in the face. The Derby Tavern, which was torn down in the mid 1980s, was as much a part of our heritage as Fort York or St. James' Cathedral. Its final years saw it deteriorate into just another dive in a city full of dives.

I remember passing the old Derby towards its ultimate end and thinking you couldn't pay me to go in. I wish I had for now I know better. For 180 years the shamrock-inspired Derby Tavern served generations of dreamers. To have heard Danny Boy sung decades ago in that tavern by someone who had just arrived from Ireland after leaving his home, his land, his mother, his brother and deliver it with such utter despair and hope for a better world beyond this one, must have been mesmerizing. Even today just hearing that opening refrain, "Oh Danny boy the pipes, the pipes are calling" can make the most macho amongst us cry buckets.

Words don't have to be recited within the walls of a cathedral to be deemed meaningful; a bar will do. Next door to the site of the Derby Tavern sit two dilapidated and boarded up houses. Maybe nothing of earth-shattering importance ever happened there but those houses built in 1855 are probably our only link to a time that is all but forgotten. They, like the Derby tenors who never sang at the Massey Halls of this world, are slowly crumbling into the dust of time.

This was the heart of Irish town. You can cry over your Angela's Ashes or get misty eyed watching old MGM movies about the great Irish immigration that came to New York in the 1850s, but for my money give me the four corners of King and Parliament streets any day. It's real. It happened here to those who came before us.

Of all the demolished buildings that have stood in our Neighbourhood the one that fascinates me the most was a sixteenth century revival of a French château known as the House of Providence. It resided on an enormous tract of land in the block bounded by Queen, King, Power and Sackville streets and stood from 1855 to 1960. I think had it survived the carnage of urban renewal it would stand out today as a remarkable example of nineteenth-century whimsical Toronto architecture, rivaling Casa Loma, Toronto City Hall and the Gooderham (Flatiron) as the most photographed building in the city. Built by architect William Hay between 1855 and 1858 it held a strikingly ironic fairy-tale presence, rising above the then slums of a forever expanding and challenged city. But it was neither a home to an eccentric millionaire or a public office building. It was a hospital built for and by the people.

By the 1850s Toronto's meager social and charitable services were becoming almost unmanageable. This was the era of mass immigration and thanks in part to the railroad; our city was flooded with newly arrived Europeans looking for a better way of life. The majority of these immigrants arrived here with nothing but the clothes on their backs and in some cases disease ridden. At the same time Toronto was experiencing a boom and bust economy making many of the working class vulnerable to malnutrition and relying on contaminated water, which in turn lead to cholera outbreaks.

Teeming slums bursting with one-room shacks holding 30 people each began to spring up in the back alleys of our Neighbourhood. The city's answer to these problems brought on by the new industrial age was to happen in two stages. The first was to expand already publicly supported institutions with the largest of these projects being the re-establishment of the Toronto General Hospital on Gerrard east of Parliament. The second tactic was to design and build new schools, hospitals and residential homes to be sponsored by various religious groups. Inner city Irish Catholics were suffering the most. With their arrival, after fleeing the Great Potato Famine back home, Toronto's population doubled. One out of every three people living in Toronto was now Irish. Although some of Toronto's wealthiest and oldest families were of Irish descent they were Protestant and the newly arrived Catholics were not greeted warmly by the old guard. Just like back in Ireland Protestant and Catholic Irish lived separately and often took to battling in the streets. Not allowed to live anywhere near their Protestant forebears they settled instead in the then unpopulated King and Parliament area and in doing so created, with the planting of cabbages in their yards, Cabbagetown. With their arrival the Roman Catholic Church built the House of Providence to take care of their needs. Although the Sisters of St. Vincent de Paul were its administrators, it served without prejudice of religious background and for the next 100 years it provided shelter for the aged, the poor and the orphaned. The House of Providence sat in the middle of a huge park south of the still standing St. Paul's Roman Catholic Church (Power Street east of Parliament) of which it was affiliated. It was built on an H plan with wings three stories high and crowned by high dormered roofs surrounding a four-story centre block itself topped off with a high dormered roof. In a publication printed after its completion in 1858 the following was written,

"The roofage forms a conspicuous feature of the design. The treatment of this too often concealed architectural covering is singularly bold and effective, representing somewhat the style of the French roofs of the early part of the sixteenth century: sharp and truncated, terminating in a crest-railing, or tall branching, with corner standards and gilt frames."

Full clusters of chimneystacks, small turret roofs and dormer gables, give considerable variety to the outline. It was through the doors of this majestic structure that many of our neighborhood's early residents got their first true sense of Canadian benevolence and with its castle-like appearance designed to give comfort to the homesick immigrant thousands flocked. The medical functions of the House of Providence were taken over by St. Michael's Hospital on Bond Street but its continued use as an orphanage and school lasted until its ultimate destruction in 1960. The period from the late 1840's to the beginning of the twentieth century was considered Toronto's golden age of architecture. Only a handful of buildings remain from that fanciful epoch like St. James' and St. Michael's cathedrals, St. Lawrence Hall and the Gooderham building. The rest, some 20,000, were destroyed after the Second World War to make way for a newer and more modern city.

The historic House of Providence palatial or not was demolished in 1960 to make way for the Richmond Street on/off ramp to the Gardiner Expressway. Once the heart and soul of not only a neighbourhood but also entire generations, the House of Providence is now a forgotten memory wiped clean off the map and from our collective conscience. After years of driving over it I decided to walk around the Richmond Street ramp with the hope I would find some clue to its former occupant. Sadly all that remains of the sixteenth century revivalist French Chateau that at one time gave hope to thousands of destitute immigrants are a few giant trees that still line Power street. So here it once stood, you'd never know if it weren't for the trees. Regardless my mind wondered as cars and trucks rumbled around me. If only it could have been saved. If only it still stood. If only the internal combustible engine had not been invented.

If only I had been taught more of the above in the first place.

SUPERMARKET IS A TOUR OF LIFE AND DEATH

*He collapsed to his death approximately where
the bulk cookies are now kept*

In any other neighbourhood (with all due respect) a trek through a supermarket is just another chore right up there with doing the laundry. But for us pushing a shopping cart around the Front Street Market Dominion store in Market Square can be like taking a walk through history. So historic are its foundations that if you feel a chill as you breeze through the frozen foods section it might not necessarily emanate from the Lean Cuisines. The ghosts of our past surround us in every aisle, bulk-bin and checkout. In the 1820s where the fish and seafood counter now sits was once the site of The White Swan Inn, a then popular drinking establishment.

In 1826 a gentleman from the United States arrived at the inn with a collection of stuffed birds and similar items with the hope of establishing a local natural history museum. Included in his menagerie were the waxed figures of American icons including presidents Washington and Jefferson.

One night some local youths broke into the museum stole the American wax-works and hung them by their necks from the trees that stood across the street.

Next door to The White Swan, where today the Dominion's main doors now stand, once stood the entrance to the Steamboat Hotel first built in 1829.

This popular waterhole, built by eighteenth century innkeeper par excellence Ulick Howard, got its name because it had, running the whole length of the building above its upper verandah a steamboat cutout complete with paddlewheels and stacks. It was in the ballroom of the Steamboat, where the present day Dominion bakery now stands, that the political leaders of the day would often throw elaborate victory parties.

Three legitimate theatres also stood on the Dominion grounds. Where the pharmacy is now once was the site of Franks Hotel where in 1820 the first theatrical performance in York—made up entirely of local actors—took place in the ballroom on the second floor.

Back then you would enter the theatre by an outside staircase where the shampoo aisle is today. The first manager was a Mr. Talbot and his wife (known to history only as Mrs. Talbot) was the first star of the Toronto stage. Her most famous role was playing Little Pickles in a comedy of the same name.

The theatre itself was very small, the ceiling low and the orchestra consisted of a violinist named Mr. Maxwell. Running through the entire present day Dominion was the continuation of Colborne Street, then starting at Yonge and ending at Market Street. Around the location of the present-day bulk food barrels once stood the Colborne Street Theatre.

In the autumn of 1829 a murder took place that later would lead to the Rebellion of 1837. Charles French (an apprentice of William Lyon Mackenzie, publisher of the anti and all-powerful Family Compact newspaper *The Colonial Advocate*), after attending an evening at this theatre, approached the town bully named Nolan who had taken on some of French's companions a few nights before. French drew his pistol and fired at Nolan, hitting him on the right side. He collapsed to his death approximately where the bulk cookies are now kept. French then went back to his lodgings at the Black Bull Tavern (still standing at Queen and Peter) where he was arrested and later hung.

Dominion's flower shop now sits on the site of Keatings Coffee House a barn-like structure that like most buildings of the day had a stable in its rear and it was there that York's third theatre was born in 1833. It had no gallery; seats were arranged on the ground floor accommodating between 200 and 300 people and the stage was approximately where the express checkout is today.

In the 1830s the theatre was lit with candles, tickets were three cents, programs were plain slips of paper and the big draw was a musical comedy team known as Mr. and Mrs. Thorne.

Where the parking entrance to the Dominion is on Church Street once stood a very famous hotel. It was there in 1841 that James Mink, a wealthy black man and the son of American slaves who owned the hotel, offered $10,000 to any white man who would marry his daughter with the idea that such a marriage in those unenlightened times could bring her some respectability.

The man finally chosen then sold her into slavery while on their honeymoon in Niagara Falls. James Mink, together with his Scottish born white wife, rescued her from the Georgia plantation where she was labouring as a cotton picker.

James Mink, guilt ridden over what he had done, built for his daughter a huge estate on the Danforth over-looking the Don River where she lived out her life in the lap of luxury.

The hotel then came into possession of Joshua Beard in 1848, who torn it down and replaced it with a brick building using the original ground floor plan. Five years later it was leased to Azro Russell who leased the upper floors to the Knights of the Masonic Temple who in turn put on extravagant operas beginning in 1849 and lasting up until 1857 when a new Masonic Hall was built on Toronto Street. It was this hotel, known as Russell's that was for years used as a home away from home to hundreds of traveling theatrical companies.

In the mid 1880s the entire north side of Front between Church and Market streets was torn down and replaced with a string of commercial Victorian buildings much like what still exists on the south side of Front. It was also during this period that the laneway behind the Dominion was born and a street no longer on any map named Mark's Lane was laid out. This tiny laneway ran north of Front, south of Colborne between Church and Market Streets where Dominion's produce aisle is now.

On Market Street facing the present day fountain was once a small hotel called the Market Arms. Though far from being considered a first- or even a second-class hotel, this 50-room inn (torn down in 1960) was just one of hundreds of small hotels that thousands of people would call home (as some still do) before the intro-duction of public housing.

There have been over the past three centuries close to 200 buildings that have stood where the Front Street Market Dominion now stands. Within the walls of those hundreds of buildings, thousands of people have lived, worked, laughed and loved and we today now walk upon their shoulders.

MARKET LANE SCHOOL

Teacher Thomas Appleton made his mark on the poor just as Bishop Strahan made his mark teaching the children of wealthy parents.

A hundred and eighty years ago there once stood a schoolhouse where the giant maple tree now stands just outside Peter's shoe repair shop in the laneway that separates the Dominion from the Hot House Café. The Market Lane School or the Common School (today's elementary) was a small 2-storey wooden structure that had as a distinguished feature a cupola that was added onto its roof to hold the bell.

This cupola, smaller and less ornate than the one St. Lawrence Hall was to have years later, became a landmark long after the school ceased to be a place of learning.

In the early 1800s going to school for the children of early York was a luxury few parents could afford. It took legislation and taxation reform between the years of 1841 and 1871 to make the government financially responsible for educating the city's youth. By 1844 it was possible for all children to attend school but it wasn't made compulsory until 1871. In 1815 however there was one school in York, a secondary school for boys that received government support. In the Home District School that once stood on the east side of Jarvis just south of Lombard the formidable Dr. Strachan, then known as the best teacher in Upper Canada, taught 50 or so boys from York's leading families.

It would be this kind of inequality, excellent government supported schooling for the rich and nothing for the poor, that would lead to the Rebellion years later. In 1818 the establishment of a common or elementary school by government grant was introduced into York and that first school which once stood on the northwest corner of Adelaide and Jarvis had as its first schoolmaster a Mr. Thomas Appleton. In 1820 that school was commandeered by the Upper Canada Central school (evolving later into Jarvis Collegiate) and poor Mr. Appleton was out of a job. The Upper Canada House of Assembly Journals of 1828 sheds some light on what it was like to go to school in York:

"Reading, spelling and conversing at least four times a day. Examination every evening in grammar, spelling and arithmetic tables. Church catechism once a week. Classes are from 9 to 12 and from 1 to 5." The budget for the entire Upper Canada Common school system in 1828 was then around $3,000 (down from $7,000 back in 1820 and yes, there were protests) and a teacher's salary was $20 a year. It was during these unenlightened times in 1820 that our little school house was born. It sat in the middle of an orchard surrounded by a white picket fence and—amazing as it seems today—the students could gaze out on an unobstructed view of the comings and goings in the harbour, which then was a few yards away just south of Front Street.

The school shared the premises with the Masonic Hall and it was in that hall on the second floor that the Mechanic Institute, the forerunner to the Toronto Public Library system, was first formed.

Today as I walk through the same area that now possesses an astounding view of St. James' Cathedral, I think back to when this plot of land was a schoolyard and to the children of our early European settlers who called this tract a playground. In 1821 Appleton, having come to York from Yorkshire only a few years earlier and having lost his job over at the Central School, was hired on as the new teacher.

In 1822 his government grant was cut off and though he continued to teach for years to come (including a stint as Master of the Central School) his case was one of the many grievances for the radical cause culminating in the Rebellion of 1837. Most of the parents of the students who attended Market Lane School were Reformers, followers of William Lyon Mackenzie who at their core were believers in a freer and more-equitable society.

If the all-powerful Bishop Strachan was to be the educator of the sons of the wealthy ruling class then Thomas Appleton was to be his direct opposite. He was known as a kind man, held in high esteem by both his pupils and their parents and although soft spoken, he too left his mark upon his students.

There was young William McMurray who lived around the corner above his father's shop on the site of the present day King Edward Hotel. Born in 1810 he worked as a page in the House of Assembly while at the school, went out to western Canada as a missionary where he married a native woman and later upon his return became the Bishop of Niagara. He died in 1894 after living a long and prosperous life.

Another of Appleton's students was Jordan Post Jr., the son of a former New Englander and his wife Melinda. Senior Post owned the south side of King over to Bay and in doing so Jordan and Melinda streets behind Commerce Court are named after them. He was a watchmaker by trade but by 1830 was one of the richest men in York owning land in the downtown core that today would be worth hundreds of millions.

There were four members of the same Bostwick family—George, Lardner Jr., May and Margaret—who also attended the school. Their father Lardner Sr. was a wheel maker and owned an acre of land at the northeast corner of King and Yonge which he purchased for a mere 100 dollars. Lardner Sr. placed an ad in the *Gazette* Oct. 11, 1811, which unwittingly speaks of an appalling practice in our history: indentured servitude.

In those days young people with little or no money signed up to learn a trade and were kept in bondage almost akin to slavery. If they ran away from their master they, like slaves, could be hunted down.

The Lardner Sr. ad read as follows: "Ran away from the Subscriber on the 22 an Indented Apprentice to the Wheel Wright's Trade, about 19 years of age, five feet 6 inches high, light hair and weak eyes; named John Brady. All persons are cautioned not to harbor or employ him." The two brothers George and Lardner Jr. in 1833 formed the Young Men's Temperance Society. George became a carriage maker and in 1836 he moved to Yorkville where in 1850 he was appointed a magistrate.

The most popular girl in the class was Margaret Phair, daughter of William Phair who owned the Union Hotel in the then Market Square (on the site of the present day North Market). He was successor to Mr. Frank of the famed Frank's Hotel (site of the now closed Cineplex lobby) and later still, Phair owned the Bull's Head Inn at King and Church. Being as popular as she was and having had her pick of boys, many of who would grow up to be wealthy and powerful, Margaret instead married the one who had the looks but no prospects.

Famed historian extraordinaire John Ross Robertson writing in 1896, observed "that after years of struggling with the worthless fellow she became so reduced in circumstances she was obliged to take in washing."

Her brother Robert also a student of Thomas Appleton was killed during the Rebellion of 1837 when he fell off his horse near the Don Bridge.

In the Dec. 29, 1825 issue of the *Colonial Advocate* its publisher William Lyon Mackenzie pays the school a visit and writes the following:

"I availed myself of a polite invitation to witness the examination of Mr. Appleton's scholars, which took place in the schoolroom, below the Mason Lodge, Nov. 17, 1825 and the parents of the scholars were also assembled to witness this interesting scene. Master Lardner Bostwick, a boy of 11 or 12 years, repeated a piece of poetry, and was careful in his pronunciation to accentuate the words on the proper syllables. Miss Margaret Phair, an interesting little child, had allotted to her Thomson's hymn on the Seasons. Is it not an enlivening sight to see a babe whose tender limbs can scare support her fragile frame, lisping that God is ever present, ever felt?"

It just makes Robertson's vision of her later in life washing the clothes of the families of the men who chased her around the orchard all the sadder. As invaluable as he is as the pre-eminent chronicler of our early history he does Margaret an injustice in passing her off as a mere washerwoman. I came across a lone listing for a Margaret Phair in an 1856 city directory living on Ontario Street and working as a laundress.

In an 1861 directory it tells that she moved to Berkeley Street and it was there she started her own business as a seamstress.

By 1868 she had her own listing in the Toronto Business Directory where it states that she was running her own boarding house at 122 Victoria Street. Was this the same little nightingale who at one time sang for Mackenzie? Though far from having the gentile life had she married one of her school beaus she nevertheless made something of herself in a time when women weren't even considered persons.

The little school house that at one time sat in the middle of an apple orchard was soon being consumed by an ever-growing city. The Masonic lodge moved out and into the premises of Beards Hotel in 1843 that once stood where the Church Street entrance to Market Square now resides. This 4-storey hotel along with the other buildings that were springing up in the Church and Front streets area cut off the Market Lane School from the rest of the world. It went through various uses before being ultimately destroyed around 1850. In an area that is so lacking in historical markers having that majestic maple tree planted there 20 years ago has inadvertently become an admirable memorial.

A CRUMBLING CITY, A MAYOR IN DISGRACE

The title Imperial City was used to describe Toronto in the late 1800s and was due to the magnificence that was Wellington Street.

You've probably walked by it a hundred times and, like me, barely gave it a second glance. It's not as ornamentally decorated as the warehouses on the south side of Front or monumentally imposing like its neighbour across the street, The Flatiron, but the history that is woven throughout the unadorned walls of the Hutchinson Block (36-42 Wellington E.) is every bit as meaningful.

The year was 1857. The newly incorporated City of Toronto was a mere 23 years old and thanks to the railroad had just witnessed an enormous growth period. The former Town of York had become a booming metropolis filled with warehouses, churches, banks, hotels and newly arrived immigrants. In spite of this tremendous influx of people and technology Mayor John Hutchinson sat in his office on the third floor of city hall (today's St. Lawrence Market) and faced his darkest hour.

The economy, once surging, was now collapsing. The great city works project of building a "Peoples Esplanade" along the harbor fell through when the railroad threatened to build along Queen Street if they couldn't have the right of way along the harbour.

Despite a public outcry, the railroad won and under Hutchison's council received thousands of acres of land along the waterfront once destined for parkland. Regardless of the railroad's promise to invigorate the economy, the city was stagnating as the province suffered through the worst economic depression in its history. There was only one thing for the mayor to do: Resign or lose everything—his reputation, his once-thriving import business and the block of buildings that he had named for himself on Wellington Street. It was to be a dark and stormy night.

Two remembrances from those dreary times, the ongoing battle to regain the waterfront as parkland and John Hutchison's landmark, have endured. The Hutchinson Building (as it was known) is all that remains of the glory that was once Wellington Street and stands today as proof of Toronto's struggle with its past.

The north side of Wellington between Church and Leader Lane—now home to a handful of restaurants, a florist, a pizza shop, a framing store, a sushi counter, a printing shop and dozens of thriving offices—survived the crash of '57 and went on to be, by the end of nineteenth century, the financial core of Toronto.

It's where the Toronto Dominion banking empire got its start and industrial giants like George Gooderham built enormous fortunes.

If Gooderham's Flatiron building was the centre diamond, then Wellington Street was the string of pearls that made up the rest of the necklace. Buildings as glorious as anything ancient Rome could offer lined its sides.

The title "Imperial City" to describe Toronto back in the late 1800s was due to the magnificence that was Wellington Street. It should also be noted that previously it had the distinction of being the red-light district of early York.

Around 1800, Church Street was considered the outskirts of town and Wellington (then called Market Street) was an access road for farmers coming into the town to sell their produce at the Market.

The only other reason to come out this far was to visit Coopers Wharf (later re-named Maitland's) that lay at the foot of Church Street just south of Front. The wharf was the first commercial pier of early York. It's where you collected your mail, said your good-byes to old friends as they set sail to far-flung shores and where you greeted new ones. It also held the first general store in York.

The only other structures in the location were Chief Judge Scott's home at Scott and Front, the jail where the King Edward Hotel now stands and a small farmhouse on the corner of what would later become Church and Wellington where Pizza Pizza now stands. As the importance of Coopers Wharf grew, so did the area.

Peter MacDougall, a French Canadian, arrived in York in 1820 and built the little farmhouse on the corner. In 1829 the house was remodeled by John Brown and turned into a hotel named Ontario House. In 1845 it was taken over by Russell Inglis and renamed The Wellington.

As a boy while working in a restaurant in Scotland, Inglis waited on novelist Sir Walter Scott (Ivanhoe) and would later retell conversations he had with the famed Scotsman to his enthralled patrons. The hotel prospered because the area was now a stage couch terminus and the Coffin block—the predecessor to the Flatiron across the street—was annexed to the main hotel and also served as the headquarters to the William Weller

Stagecoach Co. Next to the hotel was the notorious Henrietta Lane.

Long gone, this laneway ran from Wellington up to Colborne Street where Gooderham Court, the condo complex that houses Wine Workshop now stands. Notorious because the street was filled with brothels and was ground zero for the first cholera epidemic. Not surprising considering it was just steps away from the harbour.

Next to Henrietta lane was John Grantham's livery stable and behind that in the Big Field, as it was known, was the winter quarters of George Bernard's Circus.

In the 1840s the area had the look and feel of a wild-west town complete with saloons, prostitutes, wooden sidewalks and horses stuck in the mud.

The area was so abundant with mud, partly due to the closeness of Lake Ontario with its waters constantly washing ashore, that the nickname Muddy York came into being. There was a joke at the time about a man who was stuck in mud with only his head showing shouting to a friend, "Never mind me! It's the horse beneath me I worried about!"

On Dec. 28, 1841 something wondrous happened on the corner of Front and Wellington: A streetlight was installed. This newfangled gadget brought Toronto into the gas age and for the first time people were walking around at night under the fuzzy glow of this marvelous invention. The gas, made from coal, was supplied by Charles Berczy son of William (Berczy Park is named for them). His company would eventually become Consumers Gas.

By the time the 1850s rolled around the north side of Wellington no longer resembled Dodge City due to the fact that three momentous events were about to change the course of Toronto's history.

The first was the Great Fire of 1849. Its after effects are still with us in the public buildings that were erected after that disaster, like St. James' Cathedral, the Adelaide Street Courthouse and St. Lawrence Town Hall.

The second great event was that marvel of Victorian Industrialism, the railroad. With its arrival came a huge economic boom.

The third was the Great Potato Famine in Ireland when Toronto's population exploded with weary immigrants fleeing the horrors back home. It was in this climate of change that John Hutchison found himself Mayor of Toronto in 1857.

He was born in Scotland in 1817 and moved with his parents to Montreal in 1828. He went on to be employed with the mercantile firm of Torrance and Co. and in 1847 he came to Toronto where he opened an importing business on Church Street just north of Front.

For the next 10 years as his business grew, Hutchinson started to take on an active part in the political and social affairs of the city. He served as alderman for St. James Ward and was a director of the Toronto and Sarnia Railroad Co. as well as the Metropolitan Gas and Water Co..

He also became a successful dry goods merchant and, in 1854 on Wellington Street, constructed a building that he named for himself. Today it's home to, among other stores, Vines Wine Bar, as well as numerous offices on the upper levels. In 1857 John Hutchison was elected Toronto's thirteenth mayor, a foretelling sign of things to come. That same year brought the worst economic crash to hit Toronto up to that date. An observer of that depression wrote the following:

"1857 will long be remembered as the gloomiest epoch in the history of the commerce and industries of the country. Solvency and enterprise seemed to be things of the past. Mercantile houses of long established reputation went by the board; the factories were idle, trade was stagnant, and the streets swarmed with beggars and vagrants. As usual, in such times of depression, drunkenness and starvation were rife and during the year close upon two thousand people were committed to gaol (jail)."

During the great depression of 1857 Hutchison resigned from office, stating that after his Wellington Street business failed he could no longer lead the city. There also was a hint of scandal. Was he, because of his directorship in the Toronto and Sarnia Railroad Co., going to personally gain from the land grants given over to the railroads?

He left the province, went to Montreal and died a bachelor five years later. (Nineteenth century historians always like to make mention of a prominent man's marital status or lack thereof.) His row of buildings were left abandoned for a few years until the boom came once again when the entire block was taken over by Boyd and Arthur's wholesale grocers. Around this time a major alteration took place. If you stand across the street and look up at the top you can see a row of small half windows starting at number 36 at the corner of Leader Lane.

At number 42 Wellington—now home to Wilson Stationary—these windows became full size after the roof was raised. From 1867 to at least 1893 the first floor and basement of number 42 was home to Samuel Trees and Co. the makers of saddler hardware.

According to an 1893 city directory, Samuel Trees was a first class leather maker who manufactured anything to with the horse and buggy trade, producing whips, blankets, carriage robes, brushes, chains and linen horse covers. At the beginning of the twentieth century the remaining two-thirds of the Hutchinson Block became the Bodgas Hotel.

The building next door (44, 50 and 52 Wellington), now home to Hernando's Hideaway Mexican Restaurant, is unique because behind its 1950s brick exterior is the original mid-nineteenth century building. If you peer into the foot-wide separation between it and the building next door you can see the original century-old east wall. Unfortunately its façade, unlike the Presbyterian Hutchinson, was wildly ornate and didn't fit into the hell that was known as "urban renewal."

So the entire exterior was removed and replaced with one that fit moralistically with what was going on in 1950s Toronto. Blandness equals modernism. In its day, however, this was an important address. The entrance to Hernando's Hideaway was once the home to Beal Brothers, another well known saddle and leather maker. The main entrance today to the upper floors was once the home to David Morton and Sons, manufacturers of laundry and toilet soaps. Next door was the Canada Jute Co., makers of bags.

In 1860 Russell Inglis died and his hotel, The Wellington, was demolished. In 1862 the site, now Pizza Pizza, became the headquarters to the Bank of Toronto. When built, the bank was the most sophisticated and luxurious building in the city and if it were still standing today would easily rival the Flatiron for the attention of the tourist's camera.

The construction of the Bank of Toronto and the building of the Toronto Stock Exchange (1855-1942) at Leader Lane and Wellington cemented the area's reputation as the banking capital of the province.

The Bank of Toronto was chartered on March 18, 1855 and its first offices were at 70 Church St. (now a parking lot) and were still standing until recently. The bank's first president was George Gooderham whose family owned Gooderham and Worts distillery.

In 1884 a 3-storey office building was built next door to make more office space for Gooderham. Today the site of this building, which was almost as opulent as the bank, is part of the L-shaped condo complex Gooderham Court whose main entrance is on Church street.

When the Flatiron building went up in 1892 Gooderham moved his offices there. In 1901 the bank was getting overcrowded and there was no room for any more alterations. The Bank of Toronto began to plan a move into what is regarded the most beautiful building Toronto ever knew, its new headquarters on the corner of King and Bay (1911-1962).

When the army of bulldozers swept through the old downtown core in the late 1950s and early '60s, one of the first gemstones to be eradicated from the scene was Gooderham's palace. It was replaced by what was seen at the time as an award-winning design: The little TD bank that still stands in part and is now Pizza Pizza. It was, when I first saw it, one of my favorite small buildings in the city, until of course I saw pictures of what was demolished to make way for it.

During the wild 1920s and depressed '30s the area that was first a wholesale district, then the financial core, reverted back to its wholesale roots with most of the buildings being converted into warehouse space. By the 1940s the area started to decay and eventually was headed for total annihilation.

Entire city blocks including the land where Berczy Park now sits and the north and south sides of Wellington where enormous warehouses, banks, stores and hotels once thrived were bulldozed under. I don't know why the Hutchinson block managed to survive the chaos that was "urban renewal" of the 1960s. Maybe because its commonplaceness and ordinary façade it managed to blend in to the background. Each epoch likes to tear down what the previous civilization built as monuments to themselves.

So much over the years has been replaced with the mindsets of that era's architects. A nondescript appearance seems to be unthreatening. Today developer Andrew Clarke, who is every bit as heritage-conscious as the late Philip Grey was, owns the Hutchison and is very much a part of the buildings legendary history. His office on the second floor, as is the rest of the interior, is completely renovated with beautifully polished wood floors and exposed brick walls.

I told him I'd like to see the years of exterior paint removed so we could appreciate the intricate brickwork that lay underneath. He tells me it's probably the paint that has saved the bricks by holding them together. Sandblasting the bricks would probably damage them but he is considering re-painting the exterior. What completely intrigues me about Mr. Clarke, a man now in his early 50s, is that he has worked in that same office since he was a boy of 12.

Back in the 1950s his father, William T. Clarke, owned a china and glass import business on the second floor and Andrew was one of his stock boys who would unpack dishes in the storeroom. His father moved out the building in 1963 and in 1983—after years of buying, renovating and selling heritage properties—the opportunity of acquiring the Hutchinson arose. Maybe out of sentimental reasons he bought the building and converted the old stockroom into his office.

Andrew tells me that just before it was eradicated from the map, Wellington Street was becoming a dark corridor. The grand palaces that lined its sidewalks, having seen better days, were beginning to crumple and their white marble facades blackened with years of soot and grime. The Imperial City was to be no more. As we sat talking in Andrew's office I couldn't help imagining what it must have been like for Mayor Hutchison during those final days as he walked through these same rooms. With his business crumpling and the city devastated with economic strife did he think he would ever return? He never did. Though he is forgotten, the building that once bore his name—unlike everything else around it—remains.

Bruce Bell

Bruce Bell

ON A 'GOOD DAY' MEN AND BOYS WERE HANGED

200 years ago you could swing for monumental crimes like falling asleep on the sidewalk or wearing a disguise in the forest.

On the north side of King between Church and Toronto streets there is such a ghastly yet riveting history that if you happen to live or work in the buildings that now occupy the site, don't read any further. You might never sleep soundly again. The two buildings, now home to Country Style Donuts on the Church street side and the CIBC on the Toronto street side, were once the site of our (York's) second court house and jail.

Between the jail and the courthouse, where the covered lane way is now, was Courthouse Square the site of the infamous gallows, where hundreds of people were hanged over a period of 15 years.

Two hundred years ago this area was considered the outskirts of town. Where the King Edward Hotel now stands stood York's first jail, far enough away from the civilized world at King and Frederick, where enemies of the state could be safely locked away in a wooden structure that looked like a fort.

That jail was getting overcrowded (it was built to hold only three people at a time) and falling apart so it was decided that a proper jail, constructed of stone, should be built.

On April 24, 1824 Lt. Gov. Maitland laid the cornerstones of the second jail and next to it a courthouse. A huge procession of judges, barristers, magistrates and other heavy-hitting citizens known as the Family Compact marched along King St. in a regal ceremony to the spot where today we line up to get our morning coffee, crullers and smokes.

The jail, with a side door on Toronto St., and the courthouse, with a side entrance on Church St., were two identical red brick buildings that sat 100 feet back facing King St. with a tunnel connecting the two underneath the hanging yard.

Prisoners charged with any degree of crimes would be thrown into the jail to await trial. There they would be bound in leather straps, thrown into a pit with straw on the floor and forced to share their cell with rats. Guards could at their will beat to death the helpless prisoner if they felt inclined to, much to the fury of the hangman who was paid per hanging.

If the prisoner was convicted a few choices were made: more jail time, banishment to a penal colony such as Australia, or death by hanging.

Two hundred years ago you could be hanged for monumental crimes like falling asleep on the sidewalk or wearing a disguise in the forest.

Lying, cheating, stealing, dressing funny (and of course murder) also got you the rope. Unlike the newly formed United States, with its own horrors of injustice, we were not yet a democracy and the fates of our early citizens were held in the hands of a few judges.

Hanging day was a big deal in early York and a great source of entertainment to the early citizens. With little or no amusements, watching a thief die was something you took the kids to see.

Back then you worked very hard for very little. From sun-up to sundown, seven days a week with time off for church, life was a grind for the residents of York.

To see someone hang for stealing that loaf of bread you baked with the intention of selling it to pay your rent and feed your family was not seen as cruel or unusual punishment.

What was cruel, even to the bloodthirsty inhabitants, were the conditions of the jail (which were to change as the years went by), but death by hanging was seen as necessary. The last hangings in Toronto were at the Don Jail in 1962.

The hanging yard was the SkyDome of its day. Thousands would show up where, on a good day, you could see a dozen men drop through the trap door and—if you had a good seat—hear their necks snap. I have never read an account of any women being hanged, but hanging boys as young as 10 was not uncommon. However, not all hangings were met with cheers.

In the aftermath of the Rebellion of 1837, 12 men were hanged including Samuel Lount and Peter Matthews, two of William Lyon Mackenzie's most arduous supporters. Those hangings caused an uproar and not only from the citizens of York.

Thousands throughout Upper Canada had signed a petition for clemency and despite explicit warnings for moderation from the British government in London, Sir George Arthur the lieutenant governor went ahead and hanged these two men in an act of what was then thought of as judicial murder.

When news of the hangings made its way to London the colonial office decreed that all further hangings were to be halted and the rest of Mackenzie's supporters were shipped off to Australia. Mackenzie himself went into exile in the United States for 10 years before returning to a hero's welcome.

Before the Rebellion, the Family Compact's rule was unchallenged. A few years after we had become a democracy, the two Canadas were united and responsible government came into being. No wonder the citizens of Toronto were willing to die for this man and the freedom he promised.

It would seem being hanged for taking part in the overthrowing of a government was seen as unjust but being executed for lifting a loaf of bread was justified.

Somewhere in what is now the entrance to the car garage behind the present site, there took place a drama Victor Hugo could have written.

A prisoner, probably a poor farmer who had supported Mackenzie in his just cause of Us vs. Them, sat for a year in a damp cell awaiting his execution.

His wife and children made daily journeys to stand on the courthouse steps with others waiting word on when the hanging would take place. All of a sudden a guard beats on the cell door and tells the frightened man that his life was to be spared, he was being shipped off tomorrow with the rest of "yer so-called freedom fighters."

Led out on to King St. in chains, his family pleading with the soldiers for a chance to say goodbye, the farmer boards a ship for a horrendous six-month sea voyage with the knowledge he will never return again.

In 1970 then Prime Minister Pierre Trudeau on a trip to Sydney Australia unveiled a monument to this man and the rest of the Canadian Exiles of 1840 saying that "it was a record of gratitude to those who risked their lives for our freedom."

At one time there was a historical plaque on the northeast corner of Church and King honouring the men who lost their lives during the Rebellion but along the way it got lost and no one has any record of its whereabouts.

There is nothing to tell us about the sheer horror and ultimate sacrifice that went on where today jellied donuts can be bought for a buck. It never ceases to amaze me that so many of our most historic sites are now covered with donut and coffee shops.

Again I say, if that spot stood in America, flags, statues, plaques and honour guards would guarantee that every school child would know what went on there.

I'm not saying we should go that far, but when the parliament buildings burned down for a second time, the legislature sat in that courthouse on that corner from 1826 to 1832. This alone should merit a slab of inscribed marble.

Similarly, the stone medallion inscribed with the two ships, the St. Lawrence and the Griffin (on the northeast corner of Front and Jarvis), was once part of a larger bas relief mural called Memorial Arch in Niagara Falls. Constructed in 1938 and commemorating the history of Canada and the heroes of the 1837 Rebellion, it was dismantled in 1967, our centennial year. William Lyon Mackenzie's home on Bond St. has more of that stone mural in the back yard.

Could you see the Americans dismantling the statue of Liberty on their bicentennial? A further insult to Mackenzie and our history is the current remodeling of the William Lyon Mackenzie federal building on Adelaide St., the former post office and taxation centre.

Bad enough that a dazzling bauble of Victorian architecture was demolished (the general post office,1869-1958) to construct this monument to 1960's federalism, but to change its name to 30 Adelaide East should have had this city and Mayor Mel Lastman up in arms.

Would our American cousins allow the name change of the Ronald Reagan federal building or the Kennedy Center in Washington to be changed?

In 1840 a new jail was opened near the Gooderham and Worts distillery, and the old jail on King St. became an insane asylum. If jail time was seen as harrowing yet honourable, a stint at the asylum was a disgrace to humanity.

People deemed insane (i.e., different) were thrown naked into crowded pits and tossed food as if there were caged beasts. Across Church at the revered St. James, a bastion of the Family Compact, who after the Rebellion reigned a Tory terror on the people of Toronto, mental illness was seen as God's way of punishing those who didn't tow the line of a civilized society.

And so they languished, curled up in a corner of a congested cell, cold, crying, screaming, alone and naked, to be forgotten about then as now.

The courthouse continued to be used until 1852 when a new one (still standing today as the Courthouse

Restaurant on Adelaide St.) was opened.

The historic courthouse at Church and King became the City Theatre and for years after it was home to James Thomson's dancing academy. When Toronto entered into its golden age in the mid 1800s the area, once considered the outskirts of town, became its centre.

A new block of buildings now fronted King and a 12-story office structure went up on the corner of King and Church. The jail was incorporated into the York Chambers building that once stood on Toronto St. up until the 1950s and the hanging yard became a back alley.

If the Victorian builders gave any thought to the then recent past none was taken.

The locale was enjoying its time as the centre of town. King, east of Yonge, was the shopping mecca of its day.

The finest restaurants, dress boutiques, bookstores and hotels shared the boulevard with business leaders, bankers and stockbrokers. The Victorians had a phrase, "doing King street," which meant what shopping along Bloor St. means today: shop till you drop.

Behind the new Adelaide St. courthouse was the Court Street Firehall and police court. A magnificent jewel tucked behind the bustle of King until it was ultimately torn down in 1956 and replaced with a parking lot.

For a few years after World War II, Toronto was savouring its last days as the Methodists' emerald city.

Sunnyside beach was enjoying its final years as an amusement park before being leveled and replaced with the Gardiner Expressway. Yonge St., light-headed after opening Toronto's first cocktail bar, the Silver Rail in 1947, was about to be ripped up with the building of the subway.

A new city hall was in the planning stages and the remains of a neighbourhood once known as Macaulaytown which sat in its way was about to be wiped clean off the map.

The lush sounds of Glenn Miller and the crack of the bat from a baseball game could still be heard coming from a radio at the back of an Esso station. Boring ol' Toronto, the town where you couldn't drink, shop, play sports or ride the streetcar on a Sunday, was about to be shaken up, shoved into a tight dress and like her wayward sister Montreal, step out purse a-swingin'.

With that drastic transformation about to unfold, our Neighbourhood, once the centre of old York and the bustling centre of old Toronto, was being eyed for demolition.

When the carnage mercifully stopped in the 1970s all was lost. With the exception of a few motley bits left

POLICE STATION 1952—north side of Court St. between Church and Toronto streets. Also used as a firehall until 1887. Now the site of Courthouse Square.

over from the once majestic Victoria Row (a shopping emporium on the south side of King between Church and Leader Lane built in 1840) there is nothing left of the regal and opulent shopping emporiums that once graced King St.

However, we aren't to be blamed for all the destruction. The Edwardians, just as gifted with the wrecker's ball, demolished half the street when they built their name-sake hotel, the King Edward, in 1904. In short, the prosperous Victorians built over what the Georgians had first created.

The equally affluent Edwardians demolished what the Victorians constructed and we, like all enlightened civilizations before us, made sure nothing prior should remain standing and built a new city to suit our needs.

When I arrived in Toronto from Sudbury in the summer of 1972, I went in search of historic old York but instead all I found was parking lots.

The northeast corner of King and Church was then home to a three-level parking garage. In the 1980s the present buildings went up and the honey-glazed moved in.

On Court St., where the firehall and later a parking lot once resided, there is now a park, appreciatively named Courthouse Square, which in a round-about way makes some sort of restitution to our past by stating with sculpture that "through knowledge comes understanding." Well, that's my interpretation, anyhow.

The irony is not lost on me that a monument somewhere in Sydney, Australia—a country at odds over its Monarchist roots—honours the men who died for our freedom on a corner of King and Church. It's time we had one of our own.

Bruce Bell

SOLDIERS IN DRAG

*Our glorious love affair with the theatre maybe got its start
because this was such a boring duty post.*

In Toronto today thousands of theatrical performances take place in hundreds of theatres large and small. We are a world leader in live theatre, third after London and New York. It wasn't always like this. It took 25 years after the founding of York in 1793 before we had our first homegrown theatre troupe.

Before the Internet, cable TV, radio and movies, the citizens of York in the early 1800s could only pitch horseshoes in the summer and ice-skate in the winter with little else in between to amuse them. Scattered sporadically throughout the year were some live performances mostly at the Garrison at Fort York and in the homes of the well to do. Eventually our Neighbourhood, being the setting of early York, not only had the first theatre in Toronto but also, as the years went by, one of the biggest in the world.

The first European theatrical performance in the region probably happened during the French regime at Fort Rouille (on the grounds of the CNE) way back in 1720. A French soldier bored out of his mind after being posted in the middle of nowhere most likely got up and sang a dirty little ditty to the amusement of his equally bored comrades, maybe with a wig and makeup. When the British arrived a few years later, they probably did the same thing too, to off set months of monotony.

In 1793 Gov. Simcoe laid out the town of York and in the ensuing years, taverns began to spring up. In 1809 in one of these taverns on Dundas near present day Bay Street, the first recorded theatrical performance in York took place when a traveling group of American actors presented School for Scandal.

Thus began our long rocky relationship with the United States when it came to cultural influence. In 1820 at the popular Franks hotel (the site of the Front Street Market) the first theatrical performance made up entirely of local actors took place. What took so long for theatre to be accepted? The first generation of citizens of York were very class conscience and held steadfast to the old ways and the theatre with its wicked women and fancy men was viewed on the same scale as prostitution. It would take the second generation, the sons of these aristocrats together with the great tides of immigration to get things going.

In 1824 an editorial written in the Upper Canada Gazette proposed that a proper theatre should be built.

"The hypocritical religionists who rail against the stage should be glad to see something like a permanent theatrical establishment in this country. A stage that could be converted into a school for practical morality where virtue and vice are placed in the strongest possible point of view. A theatre where our greatest poets and men of genius could perhaps conceive a genius not less towering than the author whom he studies..."

The following year on Dec. 31, 1825 in a tavern called the Mansion House that once stood on the north side of King Street just east of Sherbourne, a British soldier attended an evening of songs given by a traveling American company. When the actors asked for requests the soldier Capt. Matthews stood up and innocently, or so the story goes, asked if they would sing the then popular but anti-British song Yankee Doodle dandy. At the time this was seen as treason and Capt. Matthews went on trial for 'Inciting the crowd into a violent act against the King'. He was acquitted a year later and that same American company stayed on till the end of January performing Shakespeare's Richard III.

Where the entrance to the Cineplex once stood in Market Square was the Colborne Street Theatre, again just a room at the back of tavern, where in 1829 a murder took place. These two events only added to the theatres' already intoxicating image. It turned the public against the idea of a proper theatre being built and put a stop to all theatrical events until 1833.

In 1834 two enterprising brothers, the Waughs, took over the former Methodist church that once stood on the corner of King and Jordan streets (just west of Yonge, there is a plaque) and transformed it into the Theatre Royal. Panoramas (where actors would stand behind opaque scrims in a tableau) were big draws and the first to be performed there was one entitled The Burning of Moscow.

In 1839 five years after incorporation a second Theatre Royal opened on a laneway behind King and York streets where the Toronto Stock Exchange now stands. It was a converted carpentry shop and only lasted a few years before being gutted by fire but it was a hit, at least with the public. A newspaper of the day The British Colonist called it "A small tenement that had recently been taken possession of a party of strolling players from Yankee land".

We really did not like Americans. According to a 175-year-old review a comedy team billed as Mr. and Mrs.

Thorne were a big draw. "Whenever they performed the house was always packed with Mrs. Thorne being an especial favorite."

By 1842 Toronto had a population of nearly 15,000 people and a barn on the north side of Front Street, where the fountain now gushes in Berczy Park, was turned into a theatre named the Deering. It didn't last long and after financial problems was converted into a restaurant.

These theatres weren't anything to write home about, with hard wooden benches for seats, candles for light and for the most part what acting was seen on early Toronto stages only slightly amused or just plain annoyed audiences.

In between the sometimes-silly melodramas and the spectacle of Moscow burning early Torontonians turned to the Opera.

The earliest known Opera staged in Toronto was The Mountaineers by Colman in 1825 at Franks Hotel. Opera had everything a town craving for excitement could want, drama, sex, comedy, sex, music, sex, colourful costumes, larger than life characters and sex.

In 1826 the Colonial Advocate (William Lyons Mackenzie's paper) wrote of its appeal: "The chief beauty of an opera is its close resemblance to scenes in real life."

In 1848 fervent non-drinker Jesse Ketchum built what could be termed as Toronto's first Opera house, Temperance Hall, on Temperance Street (one block north of Adelaide off Yonge) where the great international opera star Anna Bishop, whose scandalous life would intrigue Torontonians for years to come, made her local debut. Later that year wealthy landowner John Ritchey built the Royal Lyceum, the largest and the first fully equipped theatre in Toronto.

Finally Toronto had a real theatre, complete with a balcony, dressing rooms, footlights, an orchestra pit and the Holman troupe—Toronto's first opera company. In 1852 John Nickinson and his theatrical company arrived from Buffalo for a two-week engagement at the Royal Lyceum. His arrival marked the beginnings of the "legitimate" theatre in Toronto.

For the next quarter century, most of it under Mr. Nickinson's expert direction, the Lyceum paved the way for such great international stars such as Ellen Terry, Henry Irving (the first actor to be knighted), Lily Langtry (mistress of Edward VII) and Sarah Bernhardt to look upon Toronto as a prosperous high point of any tour.

The Royal Lyceum, where in 1861 Anna Bishop returned to spellbound Toronto audiences, stood where the Royal Trust tower now stands as part of the TD Centre and was in operation for 25 years before it was destroyed by fire in 1874. In 1875 the site became home to the Royal Opera House but it too succumbed to fire in 1883. For years after it sat as a burnt out shell, its glory days long over, while the city grew around it.

The building of the Lyceum with its state of the art facilities didn't put an end to backroom taverns being used as theatres, however. Where today the Church Street entrance is for Market Square's underground parking there once stood Russell's hotel.

The upper floor was principally used by the St. Andrew's Lodge of Freemasons where its members put on extravagant operas beginning in 1849 and lasting until 1857 when a new Masonic Hall was built on Toronto Street. On April 1, 1851 the St. Lawrence Hall (still standing) opened its doors and its musical heritage has passed into legend. In October that same year Jenny Lind, the Swedish nightingale, made her Toronto debut.

She was the first worldwide superstar rivaling the hysteria The Beatles created over a century later.

A singing phenomenon promoted by an equally revolutionary impresario, P. T. Barnum, Jenny Lind brought an unprecedented excitement to a then-mundane Toronto that was nothing less than spectacular. Also making her St. Lawrence Hall debut that year was Anna Bishop who had just deserted her husband for her accompanist. The auditorium, which could seat 1,000 people, was the pride of Toronto. In 1874 the Grand Opera House was built on the south side of Adelaide just west of Yonge Street. Quite possibly the greatest theatre Toronto ever knew, this 1,750-seat palace to the arts saw in its day the world's greatest entertainers, actors like Maurice Barrymore and Sarah Bernhardt to the magnificent Italian baritones Giuseppe Del Puente and Antonio Galassi.

The building of the Grand put an end to the 25-year reign of St. Lawrence Hall as the premiere stage in Toronto. The Grand Opera House, after suffering neglect and numerous fires, was torn down in 1927. Today the only hint of its existence is the laneway that bears its name running off Adelaide Street. Unlike today when going to the opera is going to the Opera with a capital O, 150 years ago a night at the opera also included comics singing the popular songs of the day, musical interludes, poetry readings and what was then termed as novelty acts. It all just mixed in together for an enjoyable night out ending with a rousing chorus of Rule Britannia. There were as many music halls then as there are movie houses today.

Where the entrance to the Eaton Centre now stands on Queen Street stood the 1,700-seat Shaftesbury Hall (1871-1902) and on Adelaide west of Yonge stood the Toronto Opera House (1886-1903) and next to it the Majestic Theatre, later re-named the Regent (1903-1930), and in 1899 the Empire Theatre replaced Temperance Hall. All opera, all the time.

On Oct. 24, 1881 all this would change. Theatre historians regard this date, the opening of the 14th Street Theatre in New York, as the birth of Vaudeville. Well move over Anna Bishop and make room for the seltzer bottle. Torontonians may have loved their opera but they were ecstatic for baggy pants, oversized shoes and cheap laughs.

This was an art form for its day but unlike opera, which has sustained its enormous appeal almost unchanged for 300 years, Vaudeville was dead by Nov. 16, 1932, the day the famed Palace Theatre in New York closed as a two-show-a-day house.

Vaudeville was what television is today, something for everybody with enormous mass appeal and influence. It was also crude, rude and highly racist, but it also had some moments of shear brilliance.

One of the greatest vaudevillians was Eva Tanguay, a Canadian, who stunned audiences with her big booming voice and comic timing. At her height she commanded $10,000 a week and *Variety*, the show-biz bible, said of her in 1924: "What Ruth is to baseball, Chaplin is to pictures, Eva is to Vaudeville".

Like so many of her contemporaries her name today is almost completely unknown. She died a recluse in 1947. Unless they made it in the movies, radio or television, vaudevillians are lost to time.

One Canadian who did manage to make it big both as a Vaudevillian and as a movie star was Marie Dressler, born in Cobourg Ontario in 1869. A typical Vaudeville show opened with an animal act, pantomime or acrobatic act, anything that didn't have to hold the audience's attention as they milled about looking for their seats. The headliner or featured act always appeared just before intermission and this much-coveted spot determined who was the star of the evening and therefore received top billing. The second act was much like the first but closing the show usually spelt the death knell for any performer as by now the audience, restless and ready to leave, had seen who they came to see. Toronto was considered "hitting the big time" on the traveling circuit and we had the theatres to prove it.

One of the first great vaudeville houses built in Toronto was Shea's theatre on the southeast corner of Adelaide and Yonge just north of the Macdonald's. It opened in 1891 as the Wonderland Museum and between 1892 and 1897 when it was destroyed by fire it was known as Moore's Musee theatre.

There is a plaque on the southeast corner commenting Toronto's first motion picture showing back in 1896. It was totally rebuilt and on Sept. 4, 1899 opened as the 1700-seat Shea's theatre. The opening bill had Professor Leonidas and his trained cats and dogs, Montgomery and Stone dancing comedians, Henri French juggler bicyclist, and Chas. Sweet the tramp musician, all for as low as 15 cents. In December 1905 fire once again destroyed the theatre.

The owners, the Shea Amusement Company of Buffalo, decided against rebuilding and constructed instead the fabulous Shea's Victoria on the

SHEA'S VICTORIA THEATRE 1955—southeast corner of Victoria and Richmond streets, built in 1910. Shown a few years before its demolition. Now a parking lot.

southeast corner of Victoria and Richmond.

What fascinates me today about Shea's Victoria (1910-1956) is, even though a parking lot now sits on that corner, the theatre that had 2,000 seats, two balconies and had the greatest vaudeville acts of its day perform on its stage, lies like the Titanic beneath the asphalt, in a crumbled state.

I often find myself being drawn to that parking lot and standing where the stage once was, imagining that beneath me lies the underbelly of the great theatre, the dressing rooms, the backstage, and the life that was.

Across the street where the Cambridge hotel now stands was the equally massive Tivoli Theatre. Up the street, thankfully still standing and faithfully restored, are the Elgin/Wintergarden (1913), and the Pantages.

When built in 1920 the Pantages was the largest vaudeville house in the British Empire. There is another now demolished theatre whose ultimate fate fascinates me. The Princess Theatre, built in 1896 on the south side of King Street West, had the unfortunate destiny to lie in the path of the newly constructed University Avenue and was torn down in 1930. Today as you cross University Ave you can stand on the spot where in 1907, three years after its première in Milan, Madam Butterfly was once performed.

By 1924, a century after the proposal was set forth that we should have at least one, Toronto had over 100 theatres including the colossal 3,665-seat Hippodrome on Bay Street, site of the present day city hall and the still standing Royal Alexandra where I made my less than heralded stage debut in 1973 as a chorus boy in the third act of Cinderella.

What killed Vaudeville was talking pictures. All these great theatres, including the Royal Alex for a time, were remodeled into movie houses and the performers hung up their canes. Our Neighbourhood, the site of the first theatres in Toronto, is still home to live theatre. On Front street there is the St. Lawrence Centre for the Performing Arts, the Hummingbird and Young Peoples Theatre. On Berkeley Street there is Canadian Stage Company, the Alumni theatre. The newest of the bunch is the Crest Theatre here at the Performing Arts Lodge (PAL) where some of our residents began their theatrical careers just

ALLEN THEATRE 1956—southwest corner of Victoria and Richmond; was known as the Tivoli in the 1920s. Now Cambridge Suites Hotel.

as Vaudeville was ending. It's a wonderful irony that PAL, which despite what the mainstream press may report is not an old age home for actors, lies in the heart of where theatre began in this city. Life was no easy ride for nineteenth- and early twentieth-century actors. Traveling theatre companies were usually made up of entire families being dragged across the country with no place to call their own. A neighbour of mine, Pat Scott, who comes from an acting dynasty stretching back generations, tells me she remembers as a young girl having to live at a boarding school while her parents traveled anywhere where there was work. My mother tells me that when she was a young girl in England, a destitute actress friend of her mother came to stay with them because she had nowhere else to go. The demolished theatres that at one time graced our streets were more than just places where actors, singers, dancers and comics performed; they were, like the Performing Arts Lodge, home.

SLAVERY AND TYRANT PETER RUSSELL

The price for the woman is $150. For the boy $200
payable in three years with interest from the day of sale.

My quest to know more about the origins of Abbey Lane, the side street with the Las Vegas lounge-act name that runs one block from Sherbourne to Princess just south of King Street, is the reason I got into this history-writing thing in the first place. Well sort of. Twenty-seven years ago I was a struggling actor fresh off the bus from northern Ontario, living in a $17-a-week attic of the only rundown mansion on Russell Hill Road.

Each morning I would walk down the tree-lined street to catch the streetcar that would take me to the subway, which would take me to my job at the Royal Alex. On those walks I began to wonder about how this majestic street in the heart of Forest Hill with its opulent homes got its name.

So I bought a book, the first book I ever bought on Toronto: Eric Arthur's *No Mean City*. It said that Russell Hill Road was named for Peter Russell, the president of the executive council and chief administrator of York in the years between governors Simcoe and Hunter (from 1796 to 1799) and that he lived with his half sister Elizabeth in a manor house named Russell Abbey in what is now the Sherbourne and King area.

Satisfied, I thought nothing more about it and went on with my life. Over the next 20 years I would often pick up and flip through that book looking primarily at its pictures of a Toronto that no longer existed. It wasn't until I moved into St. Lawrence Neighbourhood in 1993 (after living in practically every other neighbourhood in Toronto) that the book would take on a more-significant meaning.

Now that I was living in the area Eric Arthur wrote about, I would take the time to actually read the thing. Spellbound by its content, I had an epiphany. I, too, would one day write my own. So, with a new apartment in a new neighbourhood—and what I hoped would be a new career—I decided to start at the beginning (well, our European beginning) and went out in search of the mythical Abbey.

As I wandered around the streets my enthusiasm turned to shellshock. Not only does practically nothing remain standing from old York, but also all that is left of the estate is a tiny backwater alley that goes largely unnoticed.

Had it not been for its street sign that somehow has managed to survive, precariously clinging to its bent-over post, Abbey Lane (which is about to enter a new phase of its 200-year-plus existence with the building of the Abbey Lane Lofts) would have faded from memory decades ago. For better or worse, the more I unearthed about the Abbey and its occupants the less naïve I became about the ancestry of this city where we live.

After the British settled here in the late 1700s, Russell Abbey became the centre of political and social power in Upper Canada and its star faded almost as fast as it rose. By the time York became Toronto in 1834 it was reduced to what it is today, a forgotten relic of British colonialism, living on in name only.

However chic loft living on this out-of-the-way laneway may become, Abbey Lane holds some ghastly secrets. Those who once suffered there write its history in blood.

Abbey Lane has the unfortunate distinction of honouring the man after whom the first street I ever lived on in Toronto is also named for, the tyrant Peter Russell. Our own Ivan the Terrible. That last part might be a slight exaggeration but he was a frightful man none the less.

In February 1806 the following advertisement appeared in the *Gazette*, a local newspaper:

To be sold, a black woman, named Peggy, aged 40 years, and a black boy, her son, named Jupiter, aged about 15 years, both of them the property of the subscriber. They are each servants for life. The price for the woman is $150. For the boy $200 payable in three years with interest from the day of sale. Signed, Peter Russell.

Well, you can forget that cheery myth of Governor Simcoe freeing the slaves in 1793 upon his arrival, standing on the shores of Lake Ontario, his arm stretched out over the heads of kneeling blacks. Slavery was a fact of life in Upper Canada and it went on for decades after our founding regardless of what schoolbooks and the CBC's Canada Series may tell us.

When it was proposed that slavery be outright abolished in the province there was an outcry from men like Peter Russell who said slaves were needed due to the shortage of good labour. So a compromise was settled upon: the Act of 1793, signed by George III himself, stated that no more slaves were to be brought in to the province and that the children of existing ones could claim freedom at age 25. It says nothing about freeing the ones already held captive. Mr. Russell felt it was right to continue keeping and selling them at his will.

Russell Abbey was the name given to his estate that once took up the block bounded by King, Front, Princess and Sherbourne streets. The house itself was built in 1797 and stood on the southwest corner of Front and Princess streets with the slave quarters behind on what is now Abbey Lane.

Back then Front Street east was named Palace Street after the grand homes that once sat at the edge of Lake Ontario in the days before land reclamation.

William Berczy, after whom the park is named, was its architect and the people of early York described the house as pretentious but elegant.

Peter Russell had come to the Thirteen Colonies as a secretary to a British administrator, returned to Britain after the American Revolution where he was appointed receiver-general of Ontario in 1792 and succeeded Gov. Simcoe as chief administrator in 1797.

Supposedly the house didn't get its medieval-sounding name until after the death of Peter in 1808. One rain-swept night his sister Elizabeth was at home entertaining a group of young people when one of them remarked that the night reminded him a popular novel of the time, *The Children of the Abbey*. The name stuck and was forever after known as the Abbey or Russell Abbey.

The name was not descriptive of anything remotely Gothic, as the house was Georgian and it was merely a fanciful remark. It was built of wood, had one story and was laid out on an H plan.

By all accounts I've read Peter Russell was as pretentious as the house in which he lived. Despised and full of his own importance, God help anyone who crossed him. The first man to hang in York was Humphrey Sullivan in May of 1800. His crime: passing on a forged note worth about one dollar. Peter Russell condemned him to death.

When no one could be found to carry out the execution, Peter granted full pardon to a man named McKnight, who was also in for theft, if he would carry out the ghastly duty. While this just might be another case of that insane practice known as Colonial justice, Peter had that same day acquitted his personal friend and member of the ruling elite John Small of the murder of John White in a duel over which wife had slighted the other. The fact that family honour amongst the privileged few was placed in a higher regard than the lives of mere mortal men was to plant the seeds of the Rebellion 37 years later.

As the most powerful magistrate in the land, Peter could also throw anybody he wanted into jail including his own slaves if they, in his words, "misbehaved." If being a slave wasn't dreadful enough, belonging to Peter must have been horrific. Peter tried numerous times before to sell Peggy because, as he put it, "her impudence was bothersome". On Sept. 19, 1801 Peter Russell writes the following to Capt. Mathew Elliot. Elliot was to find a buyer or buy the slave Peggy himself.

My slave Peggy, whom you were so good to promise to assist in getting rid of, has remained in prison ever since you left but was released last week by order of the chief justice. I was obliged to pay the gaoler (jailer). She is now at large, being not permitted by my sister to enter this house and shows a disposition at times to be very troublesome, which may perhaps compel me to commit her again to prison. For though I have received no money from you for her, my property in her is gone from me while you hold the bill of sale; and I cannot consequently give a valid title to any other who may be inclined to take her off my hands. I beg to hear from you soon.

Peggy was the wife of a free household servant named Pompadour and mother to Amy, Milly and Jupiter, all slaves. Elliot gave the bill of sale to Chief Thayendanegea, known to history as Joseph Brant the principal chief of the Iroquois Six Nations who fought on the British side in the American Revolution and who, after the war, led his people to a new settlement on the Grand River. Had that sale gone through, Peggy would have been removed from her family at York and been forced to settle with Brant in the western region of Upper Canada. The sale to Brant fell though and Peggy remained in the Russell family. It is known that Russell hated and mistrusted Brant and built a blockhouse on the site of present day Gooderham and Worts to protect the town from an imagined "Indian attack" led by Brant. It's not known why Joseph wanted to buy a slave. I want to believe that Brant, knowing the ills of prejudice first hand, wanted to give her freedom.

RUSSELL ABBEY 1797—the home of Peter Russell, the tyrant of early York. Northwest corner of Princess and Front streets.

Regardless, Russell refused and the deal fell through. Was Peggy a victim of Peter's lust? Was it that he couldn't bear to be separated from her? Talk like that, let alone having it published, could have gotten me hanged back in those days. Elizabeth Russell was equally intolerant when it came to writing about her slaves. In her diary dated Jan. 18, 1806 she writes the following:

Peggy and John Beacher are the only ones we have except Milly, and they are certainly dirty, idle and insolent. John from being always at work does as little as he can help, throws most of the work he used to do on Pompadour who is hired by the day and is very indolent and dirty. Milly exactly copies their manner. Amy, who is at the farm, is rather better than her but is very wild and fond of rambling and both are very much addicted to pilfering and lying but it is all owing to the bad example their mother sets for them.

She continues on Jan. 27:

Jupiter was released from prison today and contrary was brought into the house, but was sent off home with Pompadour who was very drunk and impertinent to Peter who was very angry at Jupiter's being brought into the house. He is such a thief and covered in lice since he was released from prison. He will remain with Pompadour until he is sold.

Of the 266 people living in York in 1797, 241 were white and 25 were black. Native born were not considered people so they weren't counted and the only reason blacks were enumerated was because they were considered property.

All but a few blacks were slaves held in bondage by our founding fathers. Farmer Peter Long owned 10, William Jarvis owned 6, and Peter Russell owned another 6. William Jarvis lived across from Russell Abbey on what would become the northwest corner of Sherbourne and Adelaide in a manor home he named for himself, Jarvis House, built in 1798. In a court record dated the first of March 1811 it states, *William Jarvis of the town of York informed the court that a negro boy and girl, his slaves, had the evening before been committed to prison for having stolen gold and silver out of the desk in his dwelling house have escaped. It is ordered that the boy named Henry be re-committed to prison and the girl returned to her master.*

Just kids, no trial, being a slave was proof enough of guilt. Technically, Jarvis Street is named after William's son, Samuel Peter Jarvis, who had a larger estate named Hazel Burn right smack in the middle of what is now the intersection of Jarvis and Queen. The fact that men like Russell and Jarvis are honoured at all was an error of nineteenth century judgement and testament to its long-held racist beliefs that matters such as slave ownership need not apply when it comes to naming streets. When Peggy wasn't being sold off she would try escaping and when she did Peter began to post his warnings thorough out the town.

This one was dated Sept. 2, 1803: *The subscriber's black servant Peggy, not having his permission to absent herself from his service, the public are hereby cautioned from employing or harbouring her without the owner's leave. Whoever will do so after this notice may expect to be treated as the law directs. Signed Peter Russell. I was quite shocked to hear that Brant knowing the ills of prejudice first hand wanted to buy a slave. But I was even more shocked to learn through one of my readers that one of Brants slaves wrote a book detailing her own dreadful life with Brant.*

I don't know why the sale of Peggy to Brant fell through, but was Peggy a victim of Peter's lust? Was it that he couldn't bear to be separated from her? Mere talk like that—let alone having it published—could have gotten me hanged back in that day.

Of the scant free black men the most prominent was Robert Franklin, who came to York with Russell as a senior servant and eventually settled on a farm in York Township after being refused land on Yonge street. When slavery was completely abolished within the British Empire in 1833 there weren't many slaves left in York, unlike the massive numbers the American founding fathers had accumulated.

When those American slaves crossed the boarder via the Underground Railroad, with one of its last stops at Parliament and King Streets, they were granted their freedom but it would be decades before they were accepted fully into society.

It would be another 30 years until slavery would be abolished in the "land of the free" to the south of us. Now back to the royal twosome.

Social position in York was based on how close you were to the governor or, in Peter's case, "the president," as Elizabeth called him. For a short time (1796-1799) Peter and his half sister Elizabeth were the power couple in York.

He expanded the boundary of York out to Peter Street just east of present day Spadina and not only did he name the street but gobbled up enormous tracts of land surrounding the area for himself. It was considered social suicide (not to mention having to get up at the crack of dawn to fight yet another pesky aforementioned duel) if you didn't curtsey to his sister Elizabeth as she paraded down King Street. If you valued your life the Rules of Conduct when dealing with this imperious duet were easy enough to follow:

1) Do not pass up one of their dinner invitations
2) Run when summoned
3) Include them both in all your party invites
4) Flatter extensively
5) More flattery

Once Peter's position started to wane with the appointments of Governors Hunter and Gore, he slipped into the background and soon after suffered a stroke. He remained at Russell Abbey a virtual recluse with his sister making excuses to him why no one was coming to call. The fact was nobody liked him.

When a prominent citizen did make a visit Elizabeth was sure to write it down in her extensive journal. Maybe its just my take on the whole situation but when I read her diaries, especially the parts that deal with the time during Peter's illness, there is an air of bleakness and a constant questioning of their social isolation.

On Jan. 7, 1808 she writes: *The Governor (Gore) gave some sort of reason by way of apology for not calling on me. Mrs. Gore also apologized for not calling on me. Major Halton did not make his appearance and the Governor did not sit long with us.* Legend has it that Peter as an amateur chemist tried to treat himself with a mustard plaster on the back of his neck and drinking a quart of wine containing crushed deer antler. This is probably what killed him in the fall of 1808. Elizabeth continued on at Russell Abbey until her death in 1822. Though her prominence as the first lady of Upper Canada was long over, she did remain close to the centre of influence. She did so by aligning herself to the new power elite, the Family Compact, with the promise of leaving those ruling families her sizable and highly valuable land left to her by Peter.

In the Queen West area today Wilcox, Phoebe, Baldwin and Marie streets are all named after Elizabeth's inherited property. Amy Pompadour, the daughter of the slave Peggy, managed to reach the age of 25 and thus gained her freedom. In 1874 Henry Scadding writes of her in his book *Toronto of Old*: We ourselves, we remember, used to gaze in former days with some curiosity at Amy here in York knowing that she had once been legally made a present of by Miss Elizabeth Russell to Mrs. Captain Denison. After Elizabeth's death in 1822 the Abbey became the home to Bishop Alexander Macdonald (1762-1840) the Roman Catholic bishop for all of Upper Canada and whose permanent home was in Kingston. When he was elected to Parliament in 1831, he moved into Russell Abbey for a time to be near the centre of government at York. In the city directory of 1833/34 it reads that a "Mr. John Munn's lives in the east wing as the west wing remains empty." Sounds spooky to me. Russell Abbey then came into the possession of Robert Baldwin, the father of responsible Government, whose own boyhood home was just down the street on the corner of Frederick and Front. On Oct. 14, 1856 a fire engulfed the entire block of King, Front, Princess and Sherbourne streets thus destroying Russell Abbey.

In 1999 on Simcoe Day (an excellent excuse for the mainstream media to drag out the same tired old stories about Toronto's fun-filled early days) the *Toronto Star* reported that Donald C. MacDonald, former leader of the provincial NDP, thought that Peter Russell was more worthy of honouring on the first Monday in August. MacDonald said Simcoe was too class conscious, that he wanted to impose the British aristocracy system upon us and that we shouldn't name a holiday after him. I guess Donald C. didn't do his homework, since Simcoe for all his flaws was a pussycat compared to Russell.

A few years ago there was also talk of changing the name of Russell Hill Road because of its association with former slave owner Peter Russell. Changing holiday or street names, however inane or virtuous the intent, is not the answer. Education is. It's all history; our history.

Someone who was here longer than Simcoe and Russell put together but is not immortalized in stone was former slave John Baker who died at the age of 105 in Jan. 1871. After fighting in the Revolutionary War he came to Canada in 1792 as a slave of Colonel Robert Isaac Day. Upon the Colonel's death in 1803 (he went down on a ship with the brother of John named Simon, also a slave) he was set free and given 200 acres of land near Cornwall. He went on to serve throughout the War of 1812 where he was wounded in that bloodbath at Lundy's Lane. He received a war pension for 57 years and died in his own house on Wellington Street (or in Cornwall, depending on which book you read) after living a full, honourable and prosperous life. That's something Peter Russell never had.

Bruce Bell

IT IS ENOUGH TO MAKE YOU WEEP

Some felt, at the end of the 1950s, that these buildings were hideous eyesores and should get what they had coming to them.

The south side of Front Street between Church and Yonge is a perfect example, mistakes and all, of what mid-twentieth century developers were capable of doing with the handful of its old buildings left standing after the utter destruction of everything else around them.

In 1830 when York was still a few years away from being the City of Toronto, the south side of Front Street was open land with a steep drop to the beach below.

The hotels of the time like the Steamboat (site of today's Market Square), the Wellington (Flatiron Building) and Ontario House (Pizza-Pizza) all had second-floor verandas that would look over the lake just steps away.

Early developers constructed a few wooden buildings on stilts rising out of the water on land that now is home to Brack Electronics east of Church Street.

The cedar posts began to gray with weather and these—the first buildings ever erected on the south side of Front—didn't last very long. In spring and fall the whole area became a muddy mess and business owners, thinking Church was far too remote from the centre of town at King and Frederick, didn't bother to venture that far.

In 1830 you could have bought the entire block from Church over to Yonge for about a thousand dollars. One of the first buildings to go up east of Church was the home of Chief Justice Thomas Scott on the northeast corner of Scott (hence the name) and Front streets

Scott was the first chairman of the Loyal and Patriotic Society of Upper Canada that bestowed medals to citizens in defence of the province. In 1842 one of the first theatres in York, Deering's Theatre, went up on that site.

West of Yonge was forest, dotted throughout with the great estates of the leaders of the day. Bishop Strachan of St. James Cathedral had an enormous manor at Front and Simcoe.

D'arcy Boulton's great home The Grange still stands today looking

BOARD OF TRADE BUILDING 1954—Northeast corner of Front and Yonge. The site is now Shopsey's Deli in the EDS buil0ding.

much as it did 170 years ago and is now part of the Art Gallery of Ontario. In 1831 a colossal castle-like home, Holland House, was built on Wellington behind the present-day eastern wing of the Royal York Hotel. This was an enormous estate that had a great lawn running down to Front.

It managed to survive the great fire that roared through the downtown core in 1904 but by then it had lost all its charm and glory and was sitting cramped up against a city that was spreading its borders and so was ultimately demolished in the clean up that followed.

In 1830 the roads were muddy, the water could kill, speaking your mind could get you hung and the south side of Front remained largely under-developed until the arrival of the railroad in 1850. Then everything changed.

DUNCAN CAMERON'S HOUSE 1885—northeast corner of George and Front now the site of Rogers Video Store.

The Esplanade, newly built, was then a tree-lined pedestrian walkway built along sides the piers and wharves that lined Lake Ontario.

When the trains came their tracks were laid on The Esplanade and warehouses began to rise along Front, forever cutting off the city from the water. In 1858 the first of these warehouses, now home to a Starbucks, was built on the south side of Front, east of Church and is presently undergoing a major restoration.

In the 1870s work began on the warehouses west of Church and they too remain relatively intact. In 1871 the building that now houses Trailhead (southwest corner of Church and Front) was originally home to P.G. Close Importers and a few years later a Mr. J.W Lang opened a wholesale grocery business there. His specialty was tea imported from Japan, India and Ceylon.

To insure his tea was the very best he employed a full time tea taster, a very novel and lucrative touch. Mr. Lang's building was unique because the front door was situated on an angle at the much-coveted corner-lot of Front and Church.

During the numerous alterations the building has endured that door has long since disappeared but you can still see the rounded corner where it once was. The building's original exterior was removed in 1960 and replaced with a layer of glazed white bricks. In 1970 stucco was applied and the painted-on relief work we see today was added.

Inside Trailhead, however, you can still see the original nineteenth century interior brickwork rising up from the floor to meet massive wooden beams that criss-cross the ceiling.

The present owner Philip Greey, whose family has owned the building since it was built, would like to restore the façade back to its original look. It could prove unfeasible, for underneath all that stucco is a mass of smashed white glazed bricks, done so the stucco would adhere.

Next door, now home to the offices of *Toronto Life* magazine, Nanno Restaurant, V. Tony Hauser Photographer and Flatirons card shop, was in 1891 the import business of J.P. Clemes, the former mayor of Port Hope, Ont., who sold dried fruits and vegetables.

This small unpretentious block was built to a serve a purpose: to hold the goods a thriving nineteenth century city craved. When the wholesale business left the area, hundreds of warehouses just like it came crashing down. A few have miraculously survived thanks to heritage-conscious owners like David Walsh, the late Philip Greey and several others who could have easily replaced them with more lucrative high-rise condos. Greey also has restored the west side of Church, south of Front (the Keg and Papillon restaurants); the north side of The Esplanade west of Church (Old Spaghetti Factory and others).

In doing so he has rescued a unique grouping of once unassuming warehouses and factories from the wrecker's ball. The three buildings next door to the block that houses Trailhead are anything but unassuming. They are the most elaborate examples of high Victorian Romanticism left standing in Toronto and without these highly ornamented warehouses our city would be a poorer place.

The Dixon Building (45-49 Front St. E.) built in 1872, is Toronto's only remaining structure with a totally cast-iron façade. During the height of the industrial age anything made of steel was considered state of the art, you had to have it if you were to be considered leading edge.

At one time the whole south end of Front west of Yonge, where today the enormous, hideous, Dominion Federal Building now stands, was known as the Iron Block. Building after building all sported this new architectural innovation. The effect was to make the exterior look like carved stone, only less expensive.

On Feb. 14, 1872 a massive fire swept through the Iron Block where not only did the façades literally melt onto the street in a messy liquefied heap of molten steel, but also their heavy weight came crashing down on surrounding buildings.

The Dixon Building, originally home to Canada Vinegrowers and now occupied by Europe Bound and Nicholas Hoare (the best bookstore in Toronto), was owned by real estate tycoon B. Homer Dixon who also built the wondrous 280 Queen West between Soho and McCall streets.

Next door at the Perkins Warehouse, built in 1874 now home to Hikers Haven, you find the perfect example of what the businessmen of the nineteenth century wanted all who came to Toronto to see: prosperity in the guise of a Venetian palazzo and its effect is truly stunning.

This is a remarkable building and at one time the entire street was filled with buildings just like it. Next door the Beardmore Building (1872), now home to Frida's and yet another hiker paradise, Out There, was originally a world-renowned harness and saddle-making factory.

Its namesake, leather king George Beardmore, also built one of the most beautiful homes in Toronto, still standing on Beverly Street across from the Art Gallery of Ontario and now serving as the Italian Consulate.

What all these former warehouses share today is a stripped down, bare bricked, exposed beam ceiling, ground level interior.

You can bet your life in their day they were anything but. With dark walnut paneling and heavily detailed ceilings, their insides were as opulent as their outsides.

From 1850 on, thanks to the railroad with its easy access to the Erie Canal, New York City and the world, Toronto overtook all other cities in Canada, with the exception of Montreal, to be the richest and most influential of them all.

It had only been a mere 50 years since the time we were considered a backwater colonial outpost. In that short span, to prove to the world that we had arrived, a stunning metropolis with the look and feel of an ancient imperial city was built. These last remaining warehouses with their powerful facades still intact are a true testament to that time.

As Toronto expanded our Neighbourhood exploded with warehouses, financial intuitions, retail stores, hotels, houses, factories, train tracks and landfill. Literally hundreds of buildings sprang up in the blocks bounded by Parliament, The Esplanade, Yonge and King streets.

According to an 1879 assessment map, 80 buildings once stood where Market Square now resides and another 30 stood where the grass now grows in St. James park.

Today any place you see a parking lot, an open patch of land or a civic garden in the downtown core, a building once stood.

When the former O'Keefe Centre and the St. Lawrence Centre for the Arts went up in the 1960s, approximately 15 buildings were demolished to make room. Another 15 were also destroyed to make way for the eventual construction of the mammoth EDS building across the street.

Add to this the 20 or so that were demolished to make room for Berczy Park and you've got a total of 50 buildings gone to make way for three.

Those are just a few of the 20,000 structures that were eventually demolished in Toronto between 1955 and 1975.

One of the most magnificent adornments Front ever held was the Board of Trade building that once stood on the northeast corner of Front and Yonge where Shopsy's deli now resides in the EDS building.

With its cone-shaped roof this imposing structure (1888) was a cherished landmark and a perfect bookend to the Gooderham (Flatiron) building a few blocks east, before it was demolished in the early 1960s. For the next 20 years its site became a parking lot.

All this makes me wonder why the Gooderham, standing alone, was spared. How could the developers of the 1960s miss the monetary advantage of being able to park that one last car at the much-coveted apex of Front and Church?

Today its easily the most photographed building in the city, but in its day the Gooderham was just another marvel awash in a sea of architecture marvels.

In 1860 William Russell, a leading correspondent for the *London Times,* wrote of Toronto:

"The city is so very surprising in the extent and excellence of its public buildings that I wrote to an American friend in New York to come up and admire what has been done in architecture under a monarchy. Churches, cathedrals, markets, post office, colleges, schools, rise in imperial dignity in the city."

However, amidst the opulence and grandeur that Russell wrote of, there were horrendous and unimaginable slums. The area that today is St. James Park was the site of a horrific ghetto as was the site of our present-day city hall on Queen and the area of King and Parliament.

If it weren't for a few courageous photojournalists of the late nineteenth century who managed to take a few snaps, these areas would have gone unnoticed. The living conditions for the poor, as deplorable as they were, was not the face Toronto or any other large city at the time wanted the world to see.

Public housing was unheard of; construction was for profit, not for the needs of everyday people. So the most profitable business leaders of the day built for themselves ornate palaces, to conduct their work in.

As these grand as they were, these now-demolished yet flamboyant buildings were surrounded by a very polluted city, shrouded in the smoke that belched from the factories these men owned.

The harbour became an open sewer and the once-pristine shoreline was now a tangle of sheds, lumber piles and grain elevators. When a local enterprise grew into an empire they would abandon their earlier place of business (Church and Front) and proceed to build a new one (King and Yonge).

It would be only a matter of time before fire, weather, or just plain neglect put their former home on the path to destruction. So by the time it came to obliterate these buildings from the landscape they would have been largely left to ruin anyway.

Some felt, at the end of the 1950s, that these buildings were hideous eyesores and should get what they had coming to them. If they only had a chance at restoration the 200 plus banks, warehouses, factories, stables, hotels, stores, restaurants and churches that once made up our Neighbourhood, the old downtown core of Victorian Toronto, the effect today would have been dazzling.

And what did we get in return? Slabs of concrete like St. Lawrence Centre for the Performing Arts, breathtaking in its brutal approach to anti-architecture. This horrible addition to Front is second only to the North Market in winning the ugliest building prize in our Neighbourhood.

How many tourists take pictures of those architectural monuments to show friends back home? Had the developers of the 1960s left the façades of the original warehouses that had once stood there, the St. Lawrence Centre wouldn't stick out like a sore thumb.

To be fair, the once austere auditorium, after undergoing an extensive reno job in 1982, saw a return to a more comfortable and glamorous theatre interior that Toronto had in abundance in the 1800s, proving velvet wins over stone everytime.

The Hummingbird (formerly O'Keefe) Centre across Scott St. sits on land that in 1866 saw the construction of the Great Western Railroad Station. Architect William G. Storm constructed the entire building out of wood and overlaid its enormous arched roof with a covering of lead.

At the beginning of the twentieth century the station, having outlived its usefulness, was converted into a wholesale vegetable market. On May 17, 1952 it was destroyed by fire, thus sparing its ultimate fate of being demolished.

Like that other 1960 architectural icon, new city hall (where at one time over 100 buildings stood) the building of the O'Keefe Centre brought Toronto kicking and screaming into a more modern age. Now ironically its own fate is in jeopardy.

The dust has settled, for now, along that stretch of Front. Although most of the buildings that at one time graced the street have long gone, my anger over their destruction diminishes slightly when I walk amongst the trees in Berczy Park on a summer's night.

There is now grass beneath my feet where at one time a factory stood. For all the destruction this section of Toronto has seen there is ironically, as I sit by a gushing fountain, a sense of serenity. I'm grateful it looks as peaceful as it does, it could have been a lot worse.

In the late 1970s instead of laying out the present-day Berczy Park there was serious talk of constructing a two-level parking garage on the site and placing the park, trees and all, on the top level. Yikes! Or, sadder still, the majestic banks and the utilitarian warehouses that once made up this area could have remained standing as decayed burnt out shells.

In the end we have faired better than most with our inner city. Besides, if one of those warehouses, Tippit Richardson's, remained standing, I wouldn't be living where I do on The Esplanade.

GENTILITY REIGNED ON GEORGE STREET

In the early 1800s the four corners of King and George were considered the heart of York.

I'm time traveling again. This time I've gone back to Aug. 27 in the year 1793 and I'm standing alone on an embankment over looking Lake Ontario at the edge of an immense yet hushed forest on land that one day will become very familiar to me. Behind me breaking through the wilderness silence is the sound of an axe tearing into a great pine tree. With the exception of the now frequent felling of trees the scene is very peaceful and serene. Real Canadian backcountry. Ahhh.

The idyllic peace is once again broken, this time by a 21-gun salute reverberating off the hills and originating from a lone ship out on the bay. The guns are announcing a royal proclamation that from this day forth the name of this pleasant post by the bay (picked out by Gov. Simcoe a few months back as the site of the new capital of Upper Canada) will no longer be called by its ancient aboriginal name of Toronto but will be forever known by its new English name—York. All very official considering no one lives here yet.

I am awakened from my trance by the sound of a car backfiring. I am standing in the twenty first century on the same spot now known as the northwest corner of Front and George streets surrounded by cars, fire engines, pollution, people, taxis, bicycles, fast food and cable giants.

As I walk up George Street, now hidden in the shadow of the great metropolis that surrounds it, I find it hard to believe that as those guns boomed in the harbour this tiny street was then being laid out as the western boundary to the town of York.Over the next two centuries George street went from being compared to Boston's Beacon Hill with fine Georgian homes lining its sides to becoming an industrial wasteland filled with factories.

It not only has the distinction of being home to our first schools but it's also played a part in the myth that is Laura Secord.The street is named after the Prince of Wales who later became George IV (b. 1762, r.1820-30). It was his father George III (after which King St. is named) who signed into existence our British beginning. One of the first buildings of note to be erected on George St. was the home of the Rev. George Okill Stuart on the southeast corner of King and George. He arrived in York in about 1800 and was the town's first real minister (the first being a Lt. Smith at Fort York) and it was he who went on to build the first St. James on the corner of King and Church. Surprisingly that first church was known as the Episcopal Church in York and it wasn't until 1827 when the name St. James began to appear. It was from his house that Rev. Stuart set up the first school in York known as the Home District Grammar School (Hooray-there's a plaque) starting in 1807.

The house, part log cabin and part clapboard, went on to become by 1833 a general store operated by the jovial and much loved George Duggan who ironically was also the town's coroner while upstairs was the practice of Dr. Thomas Duggan, his brother. The house, which later became an inn stood until 1879 when the present building originally built as the Little York Hotel went up. In the early 1800s the four corners of King and George were considered the heart of York and its business district. In the Gazette a local paper dated March 18, 1822 an advertisement for the sale of the lot next to the famous house stated: "One of the most eligible lots in the Town of York, and situated in King Street, in the centre of the Town."

Next to the lot was Wragg and Co. a procurer of nails and chains. On the northwest corner was the store of Mr. Harris and on the northeast corner were the merchant E. Lesslie and Son's. On the present day northwest corner of George and Adelaide now the Goodwill store was Simon Washburn's house, he was married to the sister of Colonel James FitzGibbon. Colonel James (then Lieut.) was the officer Laura Secord gave the information to during the War of 1812. The official tribute reads as follows... "The circumstances connected with the affair at Beaver Dam where Col. FitzGibbon gained so much praise for the victory achieved by him over the Americans was owing to information which Mrs. Secord, widow of James Secord, obtained of the American troops to surround and take FitzGibbon and party."

The colonel, who lived in the Queen and Spadina area, was not only a great hero to the people of York but also to the powers that be back in England. In 1850 as a reward for outstanding service he was given his own apartment in Windsor Castle outside London, then the centre of world authority, where he lived until his death in 1863. Back at the house on George Street his sister Mrs. Washburn (unlike Mrs. Secord history has forgotten her first name) had four sons and one daughter. One of her son's was killed when the balcony of the City Hall collapsed (now the site of the North Market) and was one of several people impaled on the butcher's hooks below. The house was built in 1808 by Henry Hale and had previously been the site of his brickyard and it was from there that the bricks that built Yonge Street in the late 1700s were first made. All that on one corner and no plaque! The one building still standing from the Town of York is the Bank of Upper Canada on the northeast corner of George and Adelaide. It was first constructed in 1825 and has gone through numerous renovations over the years and it like the Post Office next to it (1833) are the area's oldest buildings and could be after Fort York and The Grange the oldest buildings still standing in Toronto.

George street north of King was the Rosedale of its day. In 1829 a Mr. Robert Manners who was a cousin of the Duke of Rutland owned one of the fine Georgian town homes that lined its east side. Later that same townhouse became a private girl's school owned by a Mrs. Crombie. It's too bad those great homes never had a chance to see old age. Factory cafeterias replaced high tea in front rooms. But it wasn't just the Industrial Revolution that destroyed old York. On the morning of April 7, 1849 Toronto awoke to a blaze that nearly destroyed the entire city. What once was an agriculturally based city of about 35,000 was quickly being consumed in a rage of fire. The centre of town bounded by King, Adelaide, George and Church streets was to change forever and along with it, the entire future of the City of Toronto.

The fire started about one in the morning in a stable behind a then-popular drinking establishment called Covey's Inn on the north side of King Street just west of George. It may have been a cow knocking over a lantern onto a pile of straw (like in the legend of the Chicago fire) or maybe a careless toss of a cigar or it could of been deliberate no one knows for sure but it grew to become one hell of a fire storm and yes there is a plaque. The aftereffects of that great fire are with us today in the way our city grew with many of the great buildings like the present St. James' Cathedral and St. Lawrence Hall being constructed. There was also talk that an enormous park be built in the centre of town stretching from King up to Bloor and from Church over to Parliament streets and that the new city was to grow around it. Of course it was never built but we did get a park that size out in the west end, High Park. The once grand east side of George street miraculously survived the great fire but eventually was torn down in 1874 to build the factory and warehouses of Christie and Brown the makers of biscuits.

In 1977 the entire block was remodeled into George Brown College. In 1907 the richly decorated Sovereign Bank on the northwest corner of George and King was built and is today incorporated into King George Square.

The row of buildings, beginning with Starbucks on the southwest corner of George and King and stretching over to Arts on King, is the oldest continuous-use block of commercial buildings left standing in Toronto.

Sections of that block date back to 1834 but over the past two centuries the entire façade has been re-done

GEORGE STREET TTC YARD 1953—West side of George between The Esplanade and Front Street, looking south from Front.

and refitted with the architectural styles of the day.

These buildings escaped the Great Fire of 1849 even though everything around them went up in flames. Over the centuries more elaborate and grandiose buildings have kissed the wrecking ball but somehow this block has managed to survive. It's almost as if they are meant to be there.

The building behind Starbucks on the east side of George Street that at one time might have been a stable, has a little sign that reads "King George's Place- since 1836." With its charming painted black wooden frames surrounding its doors, windows and continuing around the corner to King Street, this is one of the few traces of Old York left in the downtown core. Horse stables, like car parks and garages today, was on every corner or behind every block. A few have survived like the one across the street at 67 George behind the Little York Bookstore which has been renovated to accommodate a twenty-first century dot com business.

In 1833 a local entrepreneur named John Cull opened the Royal Floating Baths on the beach that one day would become The Esplanade between George and Frederick streets. In a town that had just seen the ravages of a cholera epidemic, these baths came as a Godsend. The complex was 110 feet long and 21 feet wide. It had 10 warm and 10 cold baths and the whole operation had an 80-foot promenade deck overlooking the lake. Besides being a much-needed facility, the baths quickly became the place to go and be seen. It also boasted a reading room, a drawing room and a refreshment room.

George Street south of Front the one we know today came into being after the first landfill in 1898.

From the 1930s onward it was home to a massive TTC yard where thousands of buses and streetcars came to be fixed and or demolished. Most, if not all, of the original Town of York (the area bounded by George, Front, Berkeley and Adelaide) was by the 1950s a forgotten relic of the past. Hardly anybody lived there and George Street, once a gentile part of town where you'd wear your Sunday best to visit a favorite aunt, became a heavily polluted and highly toxic factory town unto itself. But George Street survived and like the former Town of York is slowly coming back to life thanks to people coming back to live where it all started.

CHRISTIE, BROWN AND CO. 1902—the makers of biscuits on the south side of Adelaide Street E. between George and Frederick streets. Now remodeled into the present-day George Brown College, St. James Campus

WORTS BUILT ONE WINDMILL, BATTLED OTHERS

Mothers fed their babies beer, kids drank beer openly in the streets, magistrates and clergy drank on the job and no wonder, water then was filthy and tasted horrible.

The Gooderham and Worts Distillery (Trinity and Mill St. in the Parliament and Front St. vicinity) is without a doubt the best-preserved nineteenth-century factory complex in the country. What rescued its unparalleled Victorian Industrial grandeur from being demolished during the riotous heyday of urban renewal in the 1960s was the fact that it kept functioning as a distillery up until the 1990s. Its walls and cobblestone paths do not only encapsulate our Neighbourhood's lustrous history, but that too of Toronto, Canada and the British Empire. The first mill to be erected on that site was back in 1831 when James Worts, a Yorkshireman, built a windmill with a millstone to grind wheat into flour on the shores of what was then our waterfront. That first millstone is today displayed prominently on a pedestal on the grounds of the complex with a bronze plaque detailing its history.

In 1832 William Gooderham, also arriving from Yorkshire, brought with him money and 54 family members to help his brother-in-law expand the business, to be known then as Worts and Gooderham. One of the first things they did was to replace the wind-powered sails on the windmill with a steam engine after realizing the breeze off the lake wasn't powerful enough.

In 1834 James Worts, despondent over the death of his wife in childbirth, committed suicide. William Gooderham, together with his seven sons (his six daughters, like other well-bred women of the nineteenth century, were not encouraged to work) and the nephews left orphaned after the death of his sister and James, took control of the factory and re-named it Gooderham and Worts.

The "Worts" in the name of the factory is not named for James Sr. but for his eldest son, James Gooderham Worts, who took over his father's side of the business. None of the nineteenth century books I use for part of my research ever mention that James Worts committed suicide; it's only in the late twentieth century that this knowledge comes into print.

What I can conclude however, is that the people of early York looked upon James Worts as being peculiar; a Quixotic character, especially after he announced to them he was going to build a windmill. Some 40 years after Worts' death, James Beaty, an early pioneer, told friends that he came upon Worts standing in the middle of the bush, on the site that was to become the distillery, and Worts was "rambling on, apparently without purpose."

Mr. Beaty goes on to say, "brooding inside Mr. Worts' brain" seemed to be a vision for what York was capable of becoming and a windmill, though viewed as eccentric by the early upright citizens of York, was to be just the beginning. It would seem that James Worts was a tortured man ahead of his time. Mr. Worts' Windmill, with its non-functioning sails, was to become a cherished folly until it was ultimately demolished in 1856 after being severely damaged in a storm a few years before.

In 1837 the company began distilling the wheat byproducts into booze for a thirsty city. Toronto for all its soon-to-be Victorian idealism and demeanor was a saloon-laden town with a tavern for every 100 people. Beer was drunk then, like water is today. Mothers fed their babies beer, kids drank beer openly in the streets, magistrates and clergy drank on the job and no wonder, water then was filthy and tasted horrible.

Dead horses, cats, dogs, manure and daily garbage were thrown onto the ice of Lake Ontario and when the ice melted, the sewage would sink into the lake, whereupon people would drink the stuff untreated. That in turn led to cholera outbreaks, killing thousands. Beer seemed a nice alternative to death.

The 45 structures that today make up the factory site were begun in 1859, the oldest being the gray limestone gristmill and distillery that can be seen from the Gardiner Expressway. It, like the windmill had been, became a landmark at the eastern end of the harbour.

The building was state of the art when built. It housed an elevator on the south side that raised grain from rail-cars to the upper floors. At its eastern end was a 100-horsepower steam engine that ran eight sets of grindstones and the western end held the distillery apparatus. The noise inside must have been deafening. Under the supervision of architect David Roberts Sr., 500 men worked on the construction, with four massive lake schooners being used to move the stone from Kingston quarries.

The building was finished in 1860, at a cost of a then-staggering sum of $25,000, making it the most expensive building project in Toronto at the time. In 1863 the malting and storage buildings, the ones with the cupo-

BANK OF TORONTO 1870—northwest corner of Church and Wellington built in 1863 and demolished in 1961. A Pizza Pizza now stands there.

las rising from their roofs, and the massive square-shaped warehouse (now used as storage for the City of Toronto) at the corner of Trinity and Mill streets, were built.

In 1869 a keg of benzene broke open that caused a huge explosion and fire spread up the elevator shaft of the main building destroying the wooden interior (later re-built), but left the gray limestone exterior standing.

In 1870, the Pure Spirits Building, one of the most charming buildings Toronto has left from this period, was built. Made of red brick, it has French doors leading out onto a wrought-iron balcony on its second floor. Solid brick piers or buttresses, used to support tall panels of plate glass, rise above the roof, The building was used for processing extremely flammable pure alcohol and the west-facing glass wall admitted as much natural light as possible thus eliminating the need for open gas jet lamps.

Three events of the mid-nineteenth century inspired the tremendous growth of Toronto and the financial boom of the Gooderham and Worts family fortunes. The first was the Great Fire of 1849 that destroyed much of our Neighbourhood and resulted in the rebuilding of the city as we know it today. The second was the coming of the railroad, which made for easier access of products streaming in and out of the city.

The third was a fungus that ruined the crop of potatoes that sustained, however meager, the people of Ireland. Toronto's population swelled with starving Irish refugees escaping the horrors of the Great Potato Famine back home. Toronto had, before these events, a small population of about 10,000, mostly of British Protestant descent. By 1851 the population grew to 30,000, with 37 per cent being Irish. They worked mostly as servants and as labourers in the many mills, including Gooderham and Worts, that sprang up along the Don River.

The newly arrived Irish, both Catholic and Protestant, settled into the area surrounding King and Parliament streets just up the road from the distillery. This area was to expand northwards and because of the cabbages that were grown in abundance it came to be known as Cabbagetown. In 1985 J.M.S. Careless wrote in *Gathering Place, People and Neighbourhoods of Toronto* of Cabbagetown's beginnings: "Blight stemmed from the dirt, debris and fumes of factories close at hand; their industrial dumps and coal-heaps not to mention stockyards, livery stables, cow-barns and all their refuse. Other major offences were the reeking hog pens of the big William Davies meatpacking plant and the cattle herded at Gooderham and Worts to feed on used brewing mash. All this and the dangers of choked privies, overflowing cesspools and contaminated wells in a district thinly served by the civic water system." Yuck!

In 1843 William Gooderham, built the Little Trinity Church on King E. because at the time St. James Cathedral at King and Church used to charge a pews fee and many working-class Anglicans couldn't afford to pay it. The Catholics too had their own church, St. Paul's on Power and Queen E., built in 1826 and re-built in 1887 as the magnificent St. Paul's Roman Catholic Basilica that stands there now. As their fortunes grew the Gooderhams, beginning in 1885, started to build worker cottages on Trinity and Sackville streets that are still standing, but they weren't the only benevolent distilling family in the district.

In 1848 the Protestant Irish of this Neighbourhood were too poor to send their children to the upscale school at St. James and free education was years off, so brewer Enoch Turner built what is today the oldest standing school building in the city, The Enoch Turner School House on Trinity Street.

There it was a perfect English-style factory town, stench and all, on the edge of a great city. What more could a working man want? Home, factory, school, church and tavern were all within walking distance. The Gooderhams, with all their wealth and power continued to live amongst their workers in a house, now demolished, on the northwest corner of Trinity and Mill streets.

In the late 1800s as Toronto was becoming more class-conscious and the dividing lines between commercial and residential areas became more defined, George Gooderham, son of William, who had now taken over the family business, built for himself an impressive mansion (still standing) in the fashionable Annex area on the northeast corner of Bloor and St. George in 1889.

George, now in full control of the family business, developed it into a financial and commercial empire becoming not only the richest man in Toronto but in all of Ontario. As the distillery flourished he enlarged its facilities and began to expand his own interests that included the Toronto and Nipissing Railroad, Manufacturers' Life Insurance, the King Edward Hotel and philanthropic enterprises like University of Toronto and The Toronto General Hospital.

In 1882 he became the president of The Bank of Toronto (forerunner to TD Bank). What he needed now was an impressive office building. In 1891 he commissioned David Roberts Jr., the son of the architect who had built the distillery, to erect what is today the crown jewel and the most photographed structure in our Neighbourhood, The Gooderham Building, also known as the Flatiron at the junction of Church, Front and Wellington streets.

There, on the fifth floor, underneath the green cone-shaped cupola, he set himself up in an office that overlooked not only the busy intersection below but also everything and everyone of which he held command, the original Big Brother. From the ships in the Harbour to the trains on The Esplanade, to the distillery in the distance, all were within his sight. Then he had commissioned what was to become one of the great legends of our Neighbourhood, a tunnel to pass underneath Wellington Street to connect with the Bank of Toronto (where Pizza Pizza now stands). Even though it's been bricked up at both ends and cable, phone and sewer lines criss-cross it, Mr. Gooderham's tunnel still exits. When he died in 1905 his funeral at St. James' Cathedral, against his last wishes for a small affair, was one of the largest the city had seen. He was a great benefactor, builder and much-loved man to the people of Toronto who lined the streets to show their respect as his cortege made its way to St. James Cemetery.

In 1920, the distillery founded by "the famous Mr. Gooderham," as he was commonly known, and by the tragic Mr. Worts, was bought by the Hiram Walker Company. Today its ultimate fate still hangs in the air, with condos, apartments and lofts springing up around it, the Gooderham and Worts complex is used mostly as a film set and no wonder: its Old World ambiance and Hollywood back-lot atmosphere is picture perfect.

To walk around within its enclave when no one is around, as I did recently, is to journey to another era. You can just make out through the centuries old dust that is the mist of time, the young nineteenth century immigrant, standing before its main gates, lunch box in hand, about to enter his first day on the job, not knowing what to expect from this new world that lay before him.

FROM SHINPLASTERS TO LOCAL CURRENCY

*Many banks got their start in St. Lawrence Neighbourhood
so it's a fitting place to found the newest currency.*

Currencies have an interesting history in the St. Lawrence Neighbourhood, where many banks had their start. The Toronto Dollar, our most recent currency, is the first local currency to appear on the scene since the Harris Shinplaster, downtown Toronto's main currency from 1838 to 1839. It was issued by T.D. Harris, a well known sign maker at 124 King St. E."

After the War of 1812, tokens gained wide use as coins. Heaps of low-denominational tokens, imported from England by merchants hoping to promote trade in the colonies and make a profit, started to flood our streets.

Most of these tokens were nameless, having no mention of the merchant who was bringing them in.

Others, like Lesslie and Co., whose store once stood on the northwest corner of George and King, had their names stamped on tokens.

These tokens, like Canadian Tire Money today, offered shoppers a rebate on future buying sprees while at the same time tempting them to return.

When the new banks opened like Bank of Upper Canada in 1821 and Bank of Montreal in 1822 they began issuing their own notes guaranteed by their reserves of gold and silver.

That first Bank of Upper Canada was in a converted store on the southeast corner of King and Frederick streets.

The bank—seen by Reformist William Lyon Mackenzie as the corner stone of the all-powerful Family Compact and therefore an enemy of the people—moved to its new headquarters on Adelaide and George in 1825 and still stands today. The Bank of Upper Canada as an institution collapsed in 1866.

When we became the nation known as the Dominion of Canada in 1867 Ottawa assumed the responsibility for money and banking and set out to standardize the country's currency. This was the birth of the penny, nickel, dime, quarter and half-dollar pieces.

In 1868 and 1869 the Canadian government withdrew from circulation millions of United States silver coins to protect Canadian coins as the only coinage in use in Canada.

While waiting for the new 1870 coins to appear the government issued 25-cent notes which the public dubbed "shinplasters" after similar notes that were used by American soldiers to line their boots.

Money is still changing.

Today it is possible to go about one's day buying food, pay a few bills, and have a coffee without ever having to touch money.

Debit cards have replaced the need to

TORONTO DOLLARS are shown with an early government 'shinplaster' used to aid a coin shortage.

carry about cash.

St. Lawrence Neighbourhood, having seen the rise and fall of so many currencies, became the birthplace of The Toronto Dollar. Launched in December 1998 The Toronto Dollar is community money whose main purpose is to create work and income through community initiatives to help those on low incomes, unemployed or homeless.

Community currencies have become popular around the world and Toronto Dollar is a paragon of the genre.

The idea is simple. The currency is produced at the same mint as the Canadian dollar so it's physically secure.

Reliable community leaders operate the exchange between Toronto Dollars and Canadian currency, so it's financially secure.

Participating merchants accept it at par with Canadian currency, so it's economically secure.

The Toronto Dollar can be bought at St. Lawrence Market and several Bank of Commerce locations. Each time a consumer purchases a Toronto Dollar, 90 cents goes immediately into a special vault for merchants who wish to redeem them for Canadian currency.

The other 10 cents is used to finance various local charitable works as determined by the broad-based board of directors and community members.

When merchants redeem their excess Toronto Dollars for Canadian currency, the Toronto dollar is again available to be sold for a dollar, with 10 cents going back to charitable works. (The business gets 90 cents for each dollar, and can claim a tax credit of 10 cents each for promotional expenses.)

Most merchants find additional ways to use Toronto Dollars, including as pay for extra part-time help, incentives and rewards to current employees and for purchases from other merchants.

A few more jobs are created and more business accrues to merchants who accept Toronto Dollars. Everybody wins. You can't say that about every currency.

Bruce Bell

WHEN OYSTER BARS WERE BROTHELS

Of the 14 buildings that once stood on the south side of King St. between Frederick and Princess streets in 1864, six were saloons

The new condo and retail complex, King George Square (between Jarvis and George streets), and the small stretch of King Street that it will come to dominate, sits smack dab in the middle of the old centre of town. Named for England's King George III (reigned 1760-1820), King St. dates back to 1793 to the beginning of our British colonial days. So much of our early European history was forever stamped "in the name of" this king that it comes as no surprise to me that after two centuries yet another development bears his name.

George III not only signed the charter to our very existence but also bears the brunt of relinquishing the United States during the American Revolution. Here is a street that has lived up to and sustained its regal name.

It has since the outset held its position as being the prominent High Street of Toronto without ever once fading into obscurity.

The centre of town has always been the intersections where King meets whatever new street became Toronto's ever-spreading border. In the beginning it was King and Berkeley where the parliament buildings once stood.

As we grew, the city centre became King and Frederick with its fine shops, a post office and seductive oyster bars.

When we were incorporated as a city in 1834 the centre became King and Jarvis where the Market and city hall once stood.

As our own westward expansion took place the city centre became King and Church streets where the courthouse, jail and St. James' Cathedral began to rise.

GAMBLE AND BIRCHALL DRY GOODS 1885—northwest corner of King and George. Now the site of the former Sovereign Bank, part of King George's Square.

In the early part of the twentieth century King and Yonge became the hub of the great banking empires. Even today the financial capital of not only Toronto but also all of Canada is King and Bay streets.

In the beginning there was a path and above that path there was a forest. The path would eventually become Front Street and the forest above, Toronto.

The early people of our Neighbourhood, the Huron and later the Iroquois used that path (the shoreline) for centuries to cross east to west from what we now call the Don River to the Humber River.

When the Europeans arrived in the late 1700s, a plan was set out. Based on the Roman grid pattern (easier access of troop movement) the forest above the shoreline was cut in straight lines.

The original Town of 1793 was but a mere few blocks bounded by Berkeley, George, Front and Adelaide streets.

Frances Stewart, an early pioneer visiting from the Kawartha Lakes region, wrote in 1822 of early York and what was to be our Neighbourhood: "It's sunk down, cut out of a great bleak forest and a deadness hangs over the place. It makes me long for Kingston evermore."

We showed her, didn't we? So, with a new town laid out, King St. became almost over night the main road. One of the first buildings to go up was Jordan Hotel at the junction of King and Ontario streets. This was to be the most popular hotel in York.

After the burning of the parliament buildings during the siege of York in 1813, the assembly sat in the ballroom on the second floor. Where the Toronto Sun building now stands there was a great estate called Maryville Lodge.

It was built in 1796 and was home to David W. Smith, surveyor-general. It was an enormous spread, built entirely from wood and stood on 20,000 acres of land, half of York. In 1829 after a succession of tenants, it became a school then a saddle shop and was ultimately demolished in 1854.

As the town expanded, merchants jostled to get prime locations on what was fast becoming a most fashionable address. In its day King and Frederick was downtown with a capital D and the commercial heart of Upper Canada.

On the northeast corner of King and Frederick stood the first brick house in York. Built in 1810 by the fabulously wealthy and eccentric Quetton St. George, it was later used as the offices of the infamous Canada

SOUTHEAST CORNER of Jarvis and King 1890—Now the site of the Second Cup in the St. James Court condo complex.

Company. This British-based company's role was to attract settlers by preparing the land, provide employment for immigrants, make loans to settlers and promote Canadian land overseas.

They also stole land from the First Nations and gave it to whomever they chose to have it. Reformers were suspicious of the English stockholders who controlled the company from across the ocean and often attacked them in the press.

The house remained the company's headquarters until 1895 when it first became a drug factory, then a boarding house, a junk shop and finally a tenement. In 1904 it was demolished and replaced by the present seven-storey building, built for the Adams Harness Co.

Across the street on the northwest corner of King and Frederick stood the house and shop of the equally wealthy Alexander Wood, best known today for the two streets named for him above Carlton off Church St. and for the well-known fact that in the late 1700s, Mr. Wood lived his life as an openly gay man.

In a letter dated Oct. 1, 1801, Alexander writes to a friend in London asking for a servant: "I'm writing to procure me a decent young man as a servant, a lad of about 15 as you see I am having difficulty in getting one to come out here by himself. His work will be mostly indoors and not laborious. However I would not wish to point out a certain place of his employment as we must have a servant as will answer my every purpose..."

In almost every book I have on early Toronto those nineteenth century authors never fail to mention that Mr. Wood was a bachelor, almost an unheard of circumstance and worthy it would seem to constantly mention.

Absurd as it may seem today the thinking then was that a man should marry, homosexual or not; it was seen as his duty to King and Country. Even poor Oscar Wilde felt compelled to take a wife.

It was only in later years during the oppressive Victorian regime that homosexuality became a criminal offence. Per capita, there were as many gay men living in York before, during and after the War of 1812 as there are now, and most of them, including soldiers from the garrison, partied at Mr. Wood's home.

On the southeast corner of King and Frederick stood the First Bank of Upper Canada that opened in 1822 and was owned by William Allan, whose great estate, Moss Park, stood at Sherbourne and Queen. The bank outgrew its location and moved to Adelaide and George where it still stands.

The bank became William Gambles Wholesale Establishment, the first in York, then a brewery, and a boot

KING AND FREDERICK 1909—Northwest corner of King and Frederick.

store and was demolished in 1915 and the present building now home to Pasquale Bros. was built. This romantic-looking red brick warehouse/store with its Juliet balcony overlooking King St. is my favorite building in the downtown core. On the southwest corner of King and Frederick once stood William Proudfoot's Wine Shop opened in 1825. It sold more than wine, including ostrich feathers and copper tea kettles, and was one of the first general stores in York. In the 1840s in a tavern that once stood there, a scandal involving the mayor and prostitutes broke. It seemed that William Cawthra one of York's more prominent citizens was being kept awake at night by the goings on at popular "oyster bar" (as brothels were nicknamed) just up the street from where he lived.

Young gentlemen, many members of the ruling elite or Family Compact were carousing outside the bar at all hours of the night. In a couple of rooms above the Oyster Bar was one of the most popular brothels in York. The owner of the property was the mayor of Toronto, Mayor Boulton, although the property was leased to a Mr. Blaxham. Mr. Cawthra charged the mayor with running a house of prostitution and Mayor Boulton was forced to step down during the trial. At the trial, the mayor said he knew nothing of the goings on at his establishment. One of the girls gave a full account of the happenings and it had nothing to do with eating oysters. The mayor was exonerated; Mr. Blaxham lost his licence and the public took delight in the scandal as it played out in the papers. None of this seemed to curtail the citizens of early Toronto from drinking heavily. Of the 14 buildings that once stood on the south side of King St. between Frederick and Princess streets in 1864, six were saloons. In 1833 the front of the building that once stood on the south side of King between George and Frederick of what is today the Yellow Café became the first in Toronto to use the numbering system.

Before buildings had numbers they were distinguished by their colour or by signs above the door like an axe, saw, plough or sheep's head. Back then your address might have been, the third building over from the axe next to the house with the green shutters, two doors over from the red ox beside the entrance to the door with the sheep's head over it.

This type of structural branding eventually became what we now know as advertising. A few buildings left standing, after the numbering system was in place, like the former National Hotel (1876) on the southeast corner of Sherbourne and King, still have above their door a sheep's head.

When the numbering of buildings began along King St. it didn't originate at Yonge as it does now, it started the other way with no.1 being at Berkeley St. This section also saw the first sidewalks laid down in York.

The row of buildings, beginning with Starbucks on the southwest corner of George and King and stretching over to Arts on King is the oldest continuous-use block of buildings left standing in Toronto; only parts of Fort York are older. Sections of that block date back to 1834 but over the past two centuries the entire façade has been re-done and refitted with the architectural styles of the day.

Stucco has been the enemy of the building that houses Starbucks but you can still make out the original structure that lay beneath as bits of the stucco fall off. These buildings escaped the Great Fire of 1849 even though everything around them went up in flames.

Over the centuries more elaborate and grandiose buildings have smooched the wrecking ball but somehow this block has managed to survive. It's almost as if, either by divine providence or by shear luck, they are meant to be there.

It's hard to believe that George St. was once the western boundary of York, it just seems so lost today amongst the splendor of the City that encircles it.

The building behind Starbucks on the east side of George St. that at one time might have been a stable, has a little sign that reads "King George's Place—since 1836." With its charming painted black wooden frames surrounding its doors, windows and continuing around the corner to King St., this is probably the only trace of Old York left in the downtown core.

King George III (for whom I will safely assume it was named) was long dead by 1836 but someone then, like now, decided to name a building for him. This was not unusual; most of our early streets including York itself (George's son) were named for members of the British Royal Family.

In 1822 Bishop Strachan of St. James' Cathedral delivered a stirring yet foreshadowing sermon to members of the very Protestant and very British Orange Lodge. From that moment on every aspect of local government for the next 125 years came under its control. Today the Orange Lodge is a benevolent society but in its heyday, with their anti-Catholic, anti-French and anti-American rhetoric, they ruled this city.

In 1841 a murder happened in front of Coleraine House, an Inn which stood where the main entrance to King George Court now stands on the north side of King Street. After an election, in which the Orange elite not surprisingly was swept into power, a bomb was thrown into a house and a shot was fired from a window killing a man walking down the street.

For decades after, on election days, St. Patrick's Day, the Queen's Birthday and July 12 (anniversary of the Battle of the Boyne when England's William of Orange defeated the forces of Ireland's King James in 1690) rioting would break out in the streets of Toronto between Protestants and Catholics.

Up until the 1950s when Toronto saw the beginnings of a worldwide immigration boom, the Irish and the English waged turf wars that could rival what is going on in Ireland today. In fact one of our nicknames was the "Belfast of the North." One of the more viscious conflicts happened on March 18, 1878 in front of St. Lawrence Hall when thousands showed up to do battle.

Across the street on the southeast corner of King and Jarvis where Second Cup now resides there was, in the early 1800s, a cabbage patch. In 1826 a building went up that housed a tailors shop, a printing office, a grocery store and a hotel called the Crown Inn. The inn lasted 10 years before the corner was taken over by William Henderson's Grocery Store.

Upstairs *The Courier of Upper Canada* (a newspaper owned by George Gurnett, mayor of Toronto during the Rebellion of 1837) had its offices. That corner is also famous for the fact that it was the site of Toronto's first "skyscraper," the 8-storey Farmers Hotel, later known as the Bristol Apartments, built by E.J. Lennox (Casa Loma and Old City Hall) in the 1890s. For years after it was the site of a garage before becoming the present condo/retail development with the old guard-sounding name, "The Court of St. James."

Across the street on the northeast corner of Jarvis and King the Daniel Brooke Building still stands and is now incorporated into the King George Square.

Daniel Brooke was a merchant who bought the land and built a hotel and livery stable in 1833. At various times the building also housed a grocery store owned by James Austin who later founded the Consumers Gas Co. and the Dominion Bank, known later as the TD. The block was also home to *The Patriot*, a conservative newspaper.

In 1848 Daniel re-built his building to what we know today. Surprisingly it too survived the Great Fire of 1849, considering next door was Coveys Tavern where legend has it the fire started in its stables on the morning of May 19.

If Toronto had not exploded into the giant metropolis it is today and remained Muddy Little York, it might today look like Kingston or Guelph. The old town might have survived but alas, the boom did come, several times and Old York was swept away.

King Street endured better than most streets in the old town. In 1874 Christie and Brown, the cookie people, built their factory on the north side of King between George and Frederick and was later masterfully remodeled into George Brown College.

In 1879 the Little York Hotel went up on the southeast corner of George and King and today still stands as Little York Books and Café. On that corner previously stood the first public school in York, the Home District School, opened June 1, 1807.

In 1907 the richly decorated Sovereign Bank NK on the northwest corner of George and King was built. Today, thanks to more caring and informed developers and city planners, it still stands and is incorporated into King George Square.

Although the buildings of the old town are gone, that block of King St., the core of Old York, is having a revival, thanks in part to the Citizens for the Old Town 1793 committee. Their goal is to let people know, through street signs, banners and plaques that right here once stood a town known as York and we who walk her streets today are her descendants.

A PLACE TO SNIFF AIR AND TO SNIFF AIRS

*The newly created merchant class now had a place where they could
parade with their wives and children in their finery
and take in the smell of fresh lake air.*

THE ESPLANADE 1894—looking west from Princess Street.

There is probably no other street, boulevard or avenue in the GTA that has had a more diverse or checkered past than The Esplanade. Its existence was born from a majestic plan of a tree-lined waterfront promenade that, over the next two centuries, saw itself transform into an industrial nightmare before becoming what it is today, a place to call home.

The idea for a public Esplanade was formed 182 years ago this July but its creation goes back much further. About 12,000 years ago a gigantic glacier, five times as high as the CN Tower, melts away and leaves in its wake the Great Lakes and our sheltered harbour. With that great melt and the warm climate that followed, people started to inhabit this area.

The first to arrive, in about 9500 BC, were the hunter-gathers known as the Fluted Point People. Over the countless centuries that followed, Huron, Iroquois and Mississauga First Nations settled this area known to them as To'ron'to, interpreted as "Meeting Place" or "Where the waters converge," but because those early people had no written language its true translation is highly debatable. By the time the first European (a French explorer who worked with Champlain named Etienne Brule) arrived in 1615, a trail between the Humber River in the west to the Don River in the east was well worn after millennia of use. Just below that ancient path was a beach. That path became Front Street and the beach would eventually evolve into The Esplanade. In 1720 the French built a fort on the grounds of the present day CNE. In 1759 fearing a British invasion, they torched it and departed. In 1760 the British arrived to survey their newly acquired land. Like most territories in the New World, it was either God's will or the opportunity to make mega-bucks that invited a European invasion. Ours seemed to be the latter.

Toronto's fate was sealed in 1760 when British Major Robert Rogers, standing on the site of the abandoned French Fort, proclaimed, "I think Toronto is a most convenient place for a factory." By "factory" he meant trading post, but it's still an ironic statement considering what was to come. In 1788, to seal the deal, the British buy for $9,000 from the Mississauga Indians most of what was to become the GTA. This event is known as The Toronto Purchase. In 1793 Governor Simcoe arrived and the Town Of York was founded. Not really caring for the "Indian-sounding" name of Toronto it was changed to honour Frederick, The Duke Of York, second son of George the III. By 1808 York built its first substantial wharf constructed at the bottom of Church Street between the present day Old York Tower and the Performing Arts Lodge. Back then there was a

THE ESPLANADE 1894—looking east from Princess Street.

JARVIS STREET 1907—looking north across The Esplanade

shear, 20-foot drop from Front Street down to the beach. So, to make the waterfront more accessible, the grading of the embankment began and is still evident today with Church, Jarvis and Market Streets inclining steeply as they do down to The Esplanade.

Cooper's Wharf (named for its builder William Cooper) was what Pearson Airport, Union Station, The Eaton Centre and Yorkdale are today. Everything that came into York came through Cooper's Wharf. It had on it the first general store in York and a shipbuilding slip. It was the place to see and be seen and where you said your tearful good-byes to loved ones as they sailed away to far flung destinations. Cooper's Wharf survived a few name changes and expansions but by 1845 it was no more. All that remains of this once historic landmark is Cooper Street, a nondescript, empty block-long road between Loblaws and the LCBO at Lakeshore Blvd. By 1818 the harbourfront was becoming a jumble of wharves and a stroll along the waterfront was the last place you'd want to go. The once pristine beach was lost forever. Something had to be done to bring the waterfront back to the people. On July 14, 1818, a Royal Patent was granted to the owners of these wharves and the lands surrounding them: "That a walkway be built and it should be called The Mall." It was to stretch from Peter Street in the west to Parliament Street in the east and follow the line of Front Street. With that, a public Esplanade was born.

These men, the newly created merchant class who assumed a British air of aristocracy about them now had a place where they could parade with their wives and children in their finery and take in the smell of fresh lake air. Trees were planted along Front Street and the drainage pipes that used to empty right onto the beach were now discharging their untreated sewage farther out into the lake. In reality The Mall was just a strip of open ground edging on the lake and remained underdeveloped for years to come, but it served its purpose well. In 1832 Gooderham and Worts built their Mill at the eastern end of the Harbour and later added its own wharf, a church (Little Trinity on King E.) and a windmill to line up with the windmill that stood at the western end of the city on the present-day CNE grounds. This imaginary windmill line was created to establish the southern limits of all piers and wharfs built out into the Harbour, hence the naming of the Windmill Line Co-op. In 1834 the City of Toronto was founded and in 1844 opened its new city hall. The harbour, like the city, was expanding with close to 30 wharves and piers lining its frontage. Evidence of that early harbour can be found today in the huge fan window of that city hall's council chamber block now encased inside the St. Lawrence Market (1904) that at one time gave the mayor and councilmen a commanding vista of the Harbour that was just steps below. The waterfront was once again becoming an eyesore. The merchant class, many of who had homes along the water, moved away leaving behind a dingy and drab world.

Not everybody was rich enough to move away and those left behind were forced to live in cramped, deteriorating shacks that faced the backs of crumbling storehouses. Lower Jarvis Street could see 20 families jammed into a few damp rooms above a storage shed and their children compelled to scrounge for pennies in the mud below. Life for those first residents of The Esplanade, however transitory, was sheer horror.

The 1850s saw the first railway lines come to Toronto with the bulk of its tracks and first train station to be built along the waterfront. At the same time a great civic works project was also planned, the construction of the modern Esplanade as a landscaped walk and carriage drive to stretch along the harbour. The builders of the railroad, The Grand Trunk, saw it as their God-given right to also construct on the waterfront. A public outcry arose and the city council threatened to oust the railroad. The Grand Trunk was then going to build its line across Queen Street and it took an act of Legislation in 1857 to transfer the land to the railroad giving it the right of way along the harbour. Progress and the grab for cash, as always, won but the building of the Esplanade as a place for people went ahead regardless. The sharing of the waterfront must have worked because in 1873 historian Henry Scadding so eloquently wrote of The Esplanade in his book, *Old Toronto*: "A great and laudable work. It has done for Toronto what the Thames Embankment has done for London..."

In 1858 larger and more modern warehouses were needed to hold all the goods that were streaming into our city. Built along the south side of Front Street (thus cutting off the once exceptional view of the lake) they still stand today. Numbers 85 (Ra Emporium), 83 (Wonderful and Whites) and 81(Starbucks) Front Street East, all have after a recent face lift, emerged looking like they did 150 years ago. These warehouses backed out onto the piers, where horse-drawn wagons loaded with products would enter through the rear, ascend the grade and come out onto Front Street. These tunnels have long since been bricked-up except for one and we here at the Performing Arts Lodge are using it as a passageway out onto Market Street. Toronto in the mid to late 1800s had room for train tracks, wharves, piers, horse drawn wagons, industry, and an Esplanade.

To add to this, Toronto's second train station, The Great Western (1866-1952), was constructed on the site of the present-day Hummingbird Centre but The Esplanade as a Peoples Walkway along the waterfront managed to survive.

PRINCESS STREET 1907—looking north across The Esplanade.

GREAT WESTERN RAILWAY STATION aftermath of a fire 1952—northeast corner of The Esplanade and Yonge. Built in 1866 as a train station but in the early 1900s it became a wholesale vegetable market. Site of present-day Hummingbird Centre.

Then, as with all things admirable about Toronto, the end too came for the old harbour and its Esplanade. Landfill. There were five major landfills, beginning in 1890 and lasting well into the 1950s. That first land-fill brought the waters edge to where the train tracks are today, created a new harbour and transformed The Esplanade into a dockyard. Over the next 80 years it was to become an industrial nightmare and its after effects were to turn The Esplanade into, according to author Pierre Berton, the most toxic street in Canada.

The Esplanade at the beginning of the twentieth century was dominated by two giant coal and lumber yards owned by the Elias Rogers Company. At the foot of Market Street were its docks, pier and distribution Centre. Ships would unload the coal and lumber, where it would sit in massive heaps (where Old York Tower and 55 The Esplanade now stand), before being placed on trains that would run the length of The Esplanade where it would then be unloaded at the refinery at Berkeley Street.

This refinery yard was colossal, taking up the block bounded by Sherbourne, Front, Berkeley and The Esplanade and it shared its acreage with the Consumer Gas Company, still standing in part and now home to The Canadian Stage Co and The Canadian Opera Co at Front and Berkeley. Coal ran this city much as electricity does today. This was the Industrial Age and the more smoke that billowed out over a metropolis, the more prosperous it appeared. No one then (and it would be years) would dare approach a factory owner and say "Excuse me, do you think you could do something about the smell?" They would have thought you were nuts or worse, a Bolshevik. Until they were cleaned in the late 1970s and early '80s, Toronto's landmark buildings suffered through years of soot and grime turning their original red sandstone, yellow brick or white limestone facades, black.

Coal dust and thick smoke filled peoples lungs and when mixed with rain and fog the consequences became a deadly concoction as it did on Dec. 5, 1952 when a toxic cloud over London England killed 12,000 people. In Toronto, until the burning of coal was banned in the late 1950s, hundreds died each year of respiratory illnesses. The Esplanade during the first half of the twentieth century was a filthy, noxious and polluted relic of the Industrial Age. In between the two enormous Elias Rogers yards was the John M. French Varnish and Colour Factory at the foot of Jarvis, Reid and Company-dealers in lumber and shingles whose dock was at the foot of Berkeley, the Iron Works of Reid and Brown (whose foundry was at the bottom of Market Street), the bridge and elevator building firm of Medler and Arnot on Berkeley and the Dominion Foundry whose ironworks yard were also situated at the popular corner of Berkeley and The Esplanade. Besides factories, warehouses were also built, many still standing along the north side of The Esplanade and have been transformed into restaurants and beer halls. And who could forget that The Esplanade was once home to the city morgue at the foot of Frederick Street? Whatever remained of the once-promising dream of a Peoples Esplanade was lost forever amongst the grit and grime of the newly constructed industrial park. Our city prospered and hundreds of people had jobs but the environment took a beating. There was scarcely a tree or a blade of grass left standing in the area where these polluting behemoths held ground. The landfill of 1911-12 saw the creation of the Toronto Harbour Commission and the building of its new headquarters at the edge of the waterfront on Lakeshore Blvd. at the foot of Bay Street. That impressive building can still be seen today, although it too lost its lakefront in 1922 when the next landfill operation began, eventually bringing the waterfront as far south as Queens Quay. Even though rail tracks had increased 10-fold you could still walk down lower Church Street as late as 1920 (surprisingly looking much the same as it does today) and view the ships that were docked there. In 1927 the viaducts under the train tracks (known as the Toronto Grade Separation) at Jarvis, Yonge and Sherbourne were built, shearing off forever The Esplanade and the city from the lake. If you pass underneath the Jarvis Street Viaduct on your way home from Loblaws you can see etched in stone the date 1927. In 1966 Toronto historian F.H. Armstrong wrote of The Esplanade's crumbling deterioration: "The Esplanade today is so completely cut off from the lake that what was intended as the showplace of the city has become one of its most unprepossessing byways." Tony Pontieri, owner of Pontieri's Auto Centre (northwest corner of Market Street and The Esplanade—established in 1958 by his father Frank) remembers seeing as a young boy in the 1960s, trains chugging along a highly industrialized Esplanade. The structure that now houses Pontieri's (once used as an army barracks during WW2) is not only one of the oldest businesses in the area, but is one of the oldest continuous-use garages in Toronto. In the 1970s heavy industry moved out of the city, old factories came down or were remodeled, train tracks were torn up and The Esplanade as we know today was born.

City works crews, while digging at the foot of Market Street, hauled out of the ground the remains of an ancient wharf that at one time graced the old waterfront.

Like the long-ago dream of a majestic tree-lined waterfront promenade, those gigantic wooden pylons were once again seeing the light of day, but to us, that dream has simply become a place we call home.

JARVIS STREET 1952- looking north from present day Loblaws before the Gardiner Expressway was built.

THE MORGUE 1952— northwest corner of Esplanade and Frederick, known as the City Dead House when it was built in the 1870s.

SUMMER OF HELL: MUD, FLIES, STENCH, DEATH

What flows today underneath out streets in well-contained sewer pipes was then happily flowing down Front Street making its way to the lake.

The War of 1812 finally ended in 1814 and the people of York went about reconstructing their town. The Legislative Buildings at Front and Berkeley streets destroyed during the occupation, would not be rebuilt for a few years; so Parliament sat for one year (1814) in the ballroom of Jordan's Hotel (The Royal York of its day) on the south side of King between Berkeley and Princess Streets.

The shops on King St. began refilling their shelves and life was returning to normal. Relations between the United States and the people of York would take a generation to fix, if at all. There would always be a mistrust of anything American and a fear of another attack was always in the backs of peoples' minds but more importantly, the seeds of a rebellion against the British way of life were growing in the minds of some of our early citizens.

That critical but lost-cause Rebellion which eventually did erupt in 1837 and led by William Lyon Mackenzie would have to wait, for the people of York had to contend with a looming disaster that no one saw coming. The week-long occupation by American forces would later be seen as a tidy bit of unpleasantness compared to the horrific plague that was about to sweep over our streets.

It begins with a fateful entry in James Lesslie's journal of 1832. Lesslie was a druggist, stationery storeowner and, in later years, an alderman. Excerpts from his journal can be read in Edith Firth's fascinating book *Life in York 1815-1834*. He writes: "The steamship, The Great Britain, arrives with 600 passengers on board—one or two sick had been put on shore at Cobourg—two new cases of cholera reported in town today and the wife of the person who died two days ago was seized by cholera and died shortly after being taken to the hospital…"

By the time the cholera epidemic had finally left the Town of York in September of the same year, 205 reported deaths had occurred, in a town of 6,000. In today's numbers, that percentage would be 150,000 people dead in four months.

Let's set the stage of that summer in 1832. Let's say that you were then an average male citizen of York, a white male around 25 born in England and you, along with your wife, ran a small inn around the Market.

You served freshly butchered meat and cheap but thirst-quenching ale. You had a few hogs that ran wild with your dogs in the streets and you kept chickens in your front yard. Your wife would do the laundry and wash the dishes in the same water you earlier used to wash off the blood from your butchering knife.

All this water would be tossed into the street when the day was done, along with potato peels and the stuff that filled your overnight guests' chamber pots. What flows today underneath our streets in well-contained sewer pipes was then happily flowing down Front Street making its way to the lake. If the sight of it didn't make you sick, then the smell would knock you off your feet. But then you were used to it; you had to be. As romantic as old paintings are of the day, they can't capture the stench that swirled in the air.

At the other end of the town near present-day Berkeley and King streets was the town's manure dump and next to that a huge mosquito-filled marsh. So, combine the swill, the sweat, the summer's heat and humidity with a swamp just bursting to explode with insects and a steamship that's just unloaded 600 immigrants, all of whom have been exposed to Asiatic cholera, and you have the beginnings of a Summer of Hell.

The epidemic began in India in 1831 and gradually moved into Europe before being brought westward with the great tides of emigration like the one that's happening now. You, as the tavern owner, are about to experience one of those 600 passengers of the Great Britain entering your premises looking for a room.

On June 23, 1832, Lesslie writes in his journal: "The cholera increasing in Town… a Mr. Stevens, a portrait painter, took ill last night at midnight and is now no more… four new cases reported since yesterday. The communication between Montreal and Prescott is stopped. The price of opium has risen from $3 to $3.50…"

The Town of York is cut off from the outside world. Signs are posted at the outer boundaries warning people not to enter. Very little is known how the disease is spread and weird ways of preventing it began to appear. One is the burning of tar and pitch in barrels outside each dwelling. It was thought that the vapours arising from the swamp caused the outbreak.

Disguise the smell and the sickness would go away. Of course, you as a respected tavern owner do your civic duty and before you throw your sewage out onto the street you light your barrel of tar. Another means of controlling its spread was to wash the inside of your home with sulphur. Usually this was done after someone died in the house. No one had (or if they did no one listened) realized that living in such filthy conditions led to the spread of germs, but then no one had heard of germs; the word had yet to be invented.

So now back to the inn, where one of your boarders has died during the night. Cholera kills fast. You can feel as fresh as a daisy in the morning and be dead at night after a day of unimaginable sickness. Your wife and kids are starting to get feverish, your next-door neighbour has boarded up his home and the Market area that only yesterday was a lively happening place becomes a ghost town.

You wrap your dead visitor in a white sheet and don't have the time to wait for the death-cart to arrive. After all, the other guests are clamouring for their dinner and the corpse is starting to smell, even you have your limits. You take the cadaver to the corner of Jarvis and Front (where present-day Timothy's now stands) and dump it alongside the day's victims and cover him with lime.

The death-cart pulls in later that evening after a long day of picking up corpses from ditches and doorways along King St. and from the infamous fever sheds that have been erected haphazardly along the waterfront. The death cart was driven by two very different men, sworn enemies of each other: William Lyon Mackenzie, soon to be our first mayor and leader of the aforementioned rebellion, and John Strachan, the hero of the occupation and later to become a bishop.

They collect your poor lodger and bring him to the freshly dug cholera pit behind St. James' Cathedral where, if rumours are true, he's still there along with 700 other souls of Toronto's combined cholera epidemics all piled one on top of another. All the bodies of the former cemetery at St. James were moved in the mid-1800s (to make way for homes, factories and stores) to their present-day interment at Parliament and Bloor streets. But not the victims of the Pit. It's not a good idea to disturb cholera graves because it might start the epidemic all over again, or so they say.

The northern end of the old cemetery that was the Pit was very marshy and on a visit to the catacombs beneath St. James' Cathedral, some workers said with a wink, that when it rains, bits of bones of the corpses of the Pit still rise to the surface. It's all rumour, but a walk in the rain through St. James' Park takes on new meaning.

One of the areas of town that was hit the hardest was Church and Wellington streets, on a little laneway that no longer exists called Henrietta St. It ran north and south from Colborne to Wellington St. (just next to where Pizza Pizza stands today). Henrietta St. was the red light district of York and it was downright filthy, wedged between two hotels, a livery stable and a circus ground. Lesslie writes in his journal on June 28, 1832: "This morning I went up to Henrietta St. where some of the worst cases have appeared. I saw a poor man being taken out and put in the covered cart to be taken to the hospital and now he is dead. Heedless of the dangers to which Intemperance peculiarly exposes them at the present period he had been laying on one of the wharves in a state of intoxication all night!"

There was a hospital, the first in York, on the corner of John and King streets, next to the present day Princess of Wales Theatre, but you wouldn't be caught dead there (no pun intended). No running water, no one ever thought of cleaning an instrument, and scalpels were held in the doctor's mouth as he performed an operation without any anesthetic.

Doctors would simply pour enough whiskey down the patient's throat until the patient passed out, usually next to the rats and beetles that shared the operating room. If you had money and were sick, you stayed at home and the servants cared for you. If you were a merchant or a farmer, it was the family who helped each other.

Usually the woman of the house who was well-versed in time-honoured ways of helping the sick would go into the bush and collect whatever was needed to be used as medicine; like tea made from foxglove or leeches collected from the swamp for the ever-popular blood-letting ceremony. It was thought that if you drained the blood it would take the sickness with it. York's first hospital was strictly for the downtrodden and the extremely poor who had no one to care for them. If you were deemed insane, (who wouldn't be what with dead bodies all over the place?), you'd spend the rest of your days locked in a jail cell.

By September 1832, the epidemic ceased and no new cases were found. Life improved a little for the town. Garbage was now being collected for the first time; people were fined if they didn't clean up their yards and many societies were formed to care for the numerous widows and orphans.

So you (being the inn keeper and family), after miraculously surviving the cholera disaster, go back to leading the normal life you once knew: letting your hogs run wild, using the same water to take your weekly bath that you used to scrub the horse down and letting your sewage flow freely down the street to the lake. You take solace in the fact that you kept your yard relatively clean and your garbage was going to be eventually picked up.

The garbage, including dead horses, was simply thrown into the forest above present-day Queen Street where it rotted away under the summer sun. Two years later in 1834, a worse epidemic of cholera hits York and kills a tenth of the population. "Why does this keep happening?" you scream. "Aren't we doing everything possible to prevent it?" It would be years before the world woke up to the fact that this disease and others like it are caused by germs that breed in swamps and in the open sewers of cities and by the fleas that carry it to the rats that live side by side with you.

Toronto gradually started to clean up its act along with the rest of the world.

That first hospital in York grew to become Toronto General Hospital and over the years we became a world leader in health care. Our streets are no longer muddy sewage-laden pathways to disease. Cholera is still with us, in refugee camps and in the poorest parts of the world where clean water and sanitation is scarce. It strikes fast but thankfully we now know how to contain it, treat it and most importantly how it breeds. Our ancestors learned the hard way and survived.

There is a plaque on the Jarvis side of St. James Park honouring Francis Collins, an early newspaperman who, along with his entire family, died in the cholera epidemic of 1834. Out of all the people who had died, why did the city choose to honour him? After the graveyard at St. James was moved, the area that is now one of Toronto's most beautiful parks became quite built up and one of the streets that ran through there was called Francis Street, a continuation of Market Street. The city, back in the 1850s, decided to name a street after him because he was the first newspaperman to report all parliamentary discussions and debates. A fitting place for a marker, considering what may lie beneath the grassy slopes of St. James. It's just a rumour.

NORTHWEST CORNER of Adelaide and Church—1890

Bruce Bell

BERCZY WAS NEVER 'ONE OF US'

Legend says he escaped to Turkey where, disguised as a woman,
he found employment in the harem of the sultan.

I am constantly roaming around our Neighbourhood trying to imagine what it once looked liked. My mind wanders. If only I could travel back in time before Urban Renewal, before the two world wars, before the turn of the twentieth century, before democracy, before Champlain and before Columbus.

As I wait for the lights to change at Church and Front my mind tries to form a mental picture of the past. What did it look like? I walk over to Berczy Park and sit by the fountain. I look around at all the trees, the grass and the birds and think it probably looked like this. Peaceful.

Well, in reality, it looked nothing like this. Back then the area was a dense forest filled with pine trees and wild animals. But today, to have any green space in the downtown core is a blessing and when the film companies aren't around you can enjoy Berczy Park even more.

It's a shame if not scandalous that so much was demolished to make way for it but it could have been a whole lot worse.

Berczy Park (pronounced bear-tzee) is only 26 years old but is named for a man who lived in these parts 200 years ago. However, the land it occupies that pie-shaped apex is very old, formed 10,000 years ago when the great glacier retreated creating the shoreline of Lake Ontario along present-day Front Street.

THE BRITISH AMERICAN ASSURANCE COMPANY 1884—northwest corner of Front and Scott streets, just across from the Hummingbird Centre.

The first people to arrive after the retreat of the ice were the Fluted Point People coming up from the south (where Ohio and Indiana are today) around 9,500 BC. A few thousand years later the Huron First Nation arrived and it was they who termed the phrase "place of meeting" or 'to'ron'to' into Toronto.

For countless of centuries to'ron'to was a place to meet during the summer months and what is now Berczy Park was then a Huron fishing camp with a small stream running beside present day Church Street. In short,

WELLINGTON STREET EAST at Leader Lane 1867—The building at the right was the Toronto Exchange demolished in the 1940s.

GOODERHAM BUILDING 1898—Church, Wellington and Front streets.

BANK OF TORONTO 1955—northwest corner of Church and Wellington streets. Now the site of Pizza-Pizza.

the centuries to come saw the British chase away the French who chased away the Mississauga who chased away the Iroquois who chased away the Huron.

It was the British who in 1788 purchased the entire GTA area from the Mississauga in a highly controversial land-deal known as the Toronto Purchase. Attending publicly-funded Ontario schools in the 1960s, I was always taught that the Indians were better off anyway after knowing England, guns, horses and Jesus. I believed this because:

a) I had no Indian friends to tell me any different

b) I loved Christmas so why shouldn't everybody? and

c) I, too, was of English heritage

I was also taught the Spanish "conquered" South America while the British "settled" North America. So with the British firmly planted in our Neighbourhood, the area known to us today as Berczy Park began its long

SCOTT STREET 1955—seen south across Front. Now the St. Lawrence Centre for the Performing Arts.

89

metamorphosis.

The park is named for non-Brit William von Moll Berczy (1748-1813). Next to William Lyon Mackenzie (our first mayor), William Berczy is my favorite Neighbourhood resident of the past.

Named Johann Albrecht Ulich von Moll he was one of six children born to a rich nobleman in Saxony. The von Molls moved to Vienna where young William dutifully studied art and architecture but his passion was for adventure and by the age of 22 he was working as a spy in Poland.

As legend has it by the time Russia invaded Poland, William Berczy had escaped to Turkey where, disguised as a woman, he found employment in the harem of the sultan. Maybe the Sultan had too many women and never noticed him, but our hero managed to live amongst them for a year working in the kitchens after which he was bought by Hungarian bandits and went on to live with them in a cave for six months.

By 1791 after living by his wits he decided to get into the people-smuggling business. In the latter part of the eighteenth-century Germans weren't allowed to leave their country so William, using an empty ship as a decoy, gathered 60 German families and sailed for the New World. He settled first in

ROYAL CANADIAN BANK 1877—North side, east of Scott. Where the fountain now gushes in Berczy Park.

Genesee County. Then in 1794 he came with about 60 German families to Upper Canada, where he was granted Markham Township for settlement.

John Graves Simcoe, our first lieutenant governor, who once shot a 16-year-old soldier in the back of the head for being five minutes late for duty, promised Berczy 64,000 acres of land near the Rouge River. In return Berczy was to lengthen Yonge Street (first begun by Simcoe's Rangers) north to the Holland Marsh.

Famine, malaria and numerous injuries slowed progress and when Berczy failed to finish the job on time, Simcoe, who liked to call the working classes "the lower orders," refused to give him any land. Berczy ended up losing everything, his land around the Rouge and his property in York.

It didn't matter to Simcoe that Berczy and his German workers had cleared the land for the original 10-block town site, constructed 35 of the original 40 houses, built the first bridge across the Don River and constructed the first St. James Church. Simcoe wanted his street.

When the Yonge Street deal fell through in 1795 the tyrant Peter Russell (soon to be the big cheese after the departure of Simcoe in 1796) wrote to Simcoe that all of Berczy land within the town of York be sold off with the money going to the government (of which Russell was chairman of the executive council).

Being "not one of us," Berczy, the now-penniless man who built York, was thrown into debtor's prison. After his release Berczy along with his wife Charlotte and two sons William and Charles left for Montreal. He managed to eke out a living as a portrait painter and one of his paintings, that of Joseph Brant, is notable even today. In 1811 he went to New York City to try and sell his manuscript *The Statistical Account of Canada*, a book he had been working on for the past 20 years. In 1813 still in New York, he went missing. Some say he was murdered over a bad debt or that a deal went wrong. Or maybe the Sultan's men had gotten to him. A few years later his widow Charlotte had his coffin dug up but all that was in it were rocks and stones. No one knows what really happened to him.

Eventually his sons moved back to Toronto where eldest son William Bent Berczy became a member of the town council. In March of 1834 it was William who first proposed that the Town of York, now on the brink of becoming a city, should revert back to being Toronto because "it is the old, original name of the place and the sound is in every respect much better." It was Simcoe 41 years earlier who decided that the name "Toronto" was too "Indian sounding" and had it changed to the more British-sounding "York."

Younger son Charles became the founder of Consumers Gas and on Dec. 28, 1841, lit the first street lamp in front of what is now the Flatiron Building. Toronto was now officially out of the dark ages. He later went on to become Postmaster. It took almost 200 years for Toronto to pay tribute to the Berczy family. Leader Lane opposite the park was once named Berczy Street but it changed in the nineteenth century after the newspaper *The Leader* had its offices there.

Berczy Park, which opened in 1975, sits upon land that during most of the nineteenth and twentieth centuries was filled with banks, warehouses stores and hotels. By the time the 1960s rolled around they were slowly crumbling into dust and were eventually demolished (I'll write about them in a later issue).

Today this tiny park is a splendid monument to the enormous contributions the Berczy family gave Toronto. But it almost never was. In the mid 1970s when plans for the redevelopment of the area were announced an enormous 3-level parking garage with the park on the top level was proposed. If it weren't for the protests emerging from local heritage-conscience developers like the late Philip Greey—then witnessing firsthand the destruction of our Neighbourhood—that hideous structure a monument to the automobile was almost built instead.

FIRES FORGED OUR CITY

'To the west the whole sky was, as it were, a vast canopy of meteors streaming from the east.' — Henry Scadding, April 7, 1849

On the morning of April 7, 1849, Toronto awoke to a blaze that nearly destroyed the entire city. What once was an agriculturally based city of about 35,000 was quickly being consumed in a rage of fire. The centre of town bounded by King, Adelaide, George and Church Streets was to change forever and, along with it, the entire future of the City of Toronto.

It seems that every major metropolis on earth has had at least one Great Fire in its past and the resulting inferno is often looked upon as a turning point in that city's history. So monumental are these fires that we tend to capitalize the words "Great" and "Fire" when we write of them.

The Great Chicago Fire of 1871, the Burning of Atlanta during the American Civil War, the Great Fire of London in 1666, the Burning of Rome in 64 A. D. (supposedly set by Emperor Nero) and the Great San Francisco Fire that followed the earthquake in 1906 are just a few of the more famous blazes.

There were also the great wartime firestorms that laid waste to Berlin, Coventry, Hamburg and the towns that sat helpless in the direct path of the opposing armies. These cities eventually did rebuild and with the resulting reconstruction made some of them even greater. More important, however, the after effects of fire disasters have made urban areas safer, with newly adopted fire-prevention precautions and highly enforced building codes.

The Great Toronto Fire started about 1 a.m. in a stable behind a then-popular drinking establishment called Covey's Inn on the north side of King St. just east of Jarvis. It may have been a cow knocking over a lantern onto a pile of straw (like in the legend of the Chicago fire), or maybe a careless toss of a cigar, or it could have been deliberate. (Half the fires in the 1800s were set on purpose.) No one knows for sure, but it grew to become one hell of a firestorm. The flames leapt from floorboards to tin roofs to wooden sidewalks, gathering fuel along the way. It wasn't until it reached St. James Cathedral with its giant bell swaying high in the belfry (the city's fire alarm) that the residents awoke to the full impact of the fire. The heat was so intense by the time it got to St. James that the giant bell rang out only a few times before it melted and came crashing through the roof below.

In his account of the fire that destroyed the old St. James, Henry Scadding (Toronto's first great historian whose house still stands behind the Eaton Centre [I don't think so.]) wrote in his book, *Toronto Of Old*, (1873) the following passage: "To the west the whole sky was, as it were, a vast canopy of meteors streaming from the east. The Church itself was consumed but the flames advanced no further. A burning shingle was seen to become entangled in the luffer-boards of the belfry and slowly to ignite the woodwork there. From a very minute start at that point, a stream of fire soon began to rise and twine itself about the upper stages of the tower and to climb nimbly up the steep slope of the spire, from the summit of which it then shot aloft into the air, speedily enveloping and overtopping the golden cross that was there. The heavy gilt cross at the apex of the spire came down with a crash and planted itself in the pavement of the entrance below, where the steps as well as the inner walls of the base of the tower, were bespattered far and wide with the molten metal of the great bell..."

What saved the town west of Church St. was the patch of ground that surrounds St. James on its west side. The fire had nothing else to burn by the time it reached the church. Other buildings were constructed right next to each other without the protection of firewalls so that as far as the flames knew, the whole city was one big tinderbox building ready to be swallowed up. Taverns, inns, book stores, clothing outlets, homes, newspaper offices, hardware stores, dry-good emporiums, liquor shops and the Market gone in one night of unbelievable terror. The heroic fire brigade did what they could, hand pumping water from barrels atop their rudimentary horse-drawn wagons. What few fire hydrants Toronto had were in the other part of town. To make matters worse the Water Company building burnt to the ground alongside everything else in the fire's path.

The residents themselves formed a line of buckets stretching down to the lake in a desperate attempt to save what was fast becoming a lost cause. Every Great Fire is comparable to a Great Symphony. Starting slowly, building impressively, momentarily pausing as if to fade away, and then, out of nowhere, like in the final moments of Beethoven's glorious 9th, comes a magnificent and dazzling crescendo. As the fires leapt higher into the night, people as far away as St. Catherine's could see the heavens over Toronto metamorphose into a blazing swirling hue of red and orange.

Toronto, the once and future capital of the region, whose rapid rise in industry and commerce was surpassing its older, more established Upper Canada neighbours, was just as rapidly transforming itself into a burnt-out heap of absolute devastation.

If a fire of those proportions were to break out today, the area bounded by Queen's Quay, Bloor, Parliament and Bathurst would be wiped off the map. The entire financial district of Bay and King, the Eaton Centre, Union Station, the Royal York Hotel, City Hall, U of T, Queen's Park, Sky Dome—not to mention the thousands of apartments, condos, and homes—would be incinerated in an inferno of biblical proportions.

Amazingly there was only one victim of the fire of 1849: Richard Watson, a newspaper man trying to salvage what he could from the smoke-filled office of his newspaper, *The Patriot.*

Toronto changed forever after that night. The present-day St. James' Cathedral was built atop the ruins of its predecessor. The old Market, that stretched from King down to Front—home to Toronto's first city hall—was razed to make way for the opulent St. Lawrence Hall and a new Market (forerunner to the present-day North Market) was built behind it.

New laws prohibiting wooden structures in the downtown core and requiring brick firewalls between each building (many can still be seen today rising above the roofs of older buildings) were passed. There are, however, a few buildings that miraculously survived the Great Fire. The three little buildings at 107, 109 and 111 King St. East between the Sculpture Garden and Church St. still stand, as does the southern side of King East between Jarvis and George St., making that section which includes a Starbucks and Arts on King the oldest continuous-use block of buildings in Toronto.

In 1851, two years after the Great Fire, the railroad came to Toronto. An enormous building boom occurred and the city as we know it today was born. If we were then just considered an upstart colonial outpost by Empire standards before the blaze, in the few short years afterwards, we were to become the richest, most powerful city in the country, after Montreal—but eventually even they would have to take a back seat.

At the turn of the new century Toronto suffered through another devastating blaze. The Great Fire of April 19, 1904 leveled the area bounded by Melinda (just south of King), The Lakeshore, Yonge and York Streets. A total of 122 buildings went up in smoke putting 230 businesses out of commission and 6,000 people out of work. Miraculously no one died and once again Toronto re-built to become one of the greatest and most enviable cities in the world today.

Bruce Bell, the popular history columnist for the St. Lawrence Neighbourhood Community Bulletin, is also an award-winning playwright, actor, standup comedian and the honourary curator of the most photographed building in the city the historic Gooderham (Flatiron) Building.

Bruce's insights into Toronto's past have brought him legions of fans who not only read his monthly column but also regularly join him around the old downtown core as he leads them on historic walking tours.

Bruce was born in Sudbury, Ont., in 1954, arrived in Toronto in 1972 where he made his stage debut at the Royal Alexandra Theatre the following year.

In 1977 Bruce ran into old friend and comic impresario Mark Breslin who was then just starting up Yuk-Yuks comedy club. Bruce joined and for the next 20 years performed across Canada as a comedian. Bruce began writing plays as far back as 1982 but it wasn't until 1989 that he had his first big success with "I Slept with Tony Trouble" which went on tour to London, England, Scotland and Stratford, Ont.

Bruce was awarded a Year 2000 Toronto Arts Council Award for playwriting. He makes his home in Toronto at the Performing Arts Lodge.

Bruce Bell